THE Job Searcher's HANDBOOK

FOURTH EDITION

Carolyn R. Robbins

Pearson

Boston   Columbus   Indianapolis   New York   San Francisco
Upper Saddle River   Amsterdam   Cape Town   Dubai
London   Madrid   Milan   Munich   Paris   Montreal
Toronto   Delhi   Mexico City   Sao Paulo   Sydney
Hong Kong   Seoul   Singapore   Taipei   Tokyo

Vice President and Editor in Chief: Jeffery W. Johnston
Executive Editor: Sande Johnson
Editorial Assistant: Lynda Cramer
Vice President, Director of Sales and Marketing: Quinn Perkson
Marketing Manager: Amy June
Marketing Coordinator: Brian Mounts
Senior Managing Editor: Pamela D. Bennett
Project Manager: Kerry J. Rubadue
Senior Operations Supervisor: Matthew Ottenweller

Art Director: Candace Rowley
Cover Designer: Diane Lorenzo
Cover Art: istock
Full-Service Project Management: Thistle Hill Publishing Services, LLC
Composition: Integra Software Services
Printer/Binder: Courier/Kendallville
Cover Printer: Coral Graphics
Text Font: 11/13 Janson Text

Credits and acknowledgments borrowed from other sources and reproduced, with permission, in this textbook appear on appropriate page within text.

Every effort has been made to provide accurate and current Internet information in this book. However, the Internet and information posted on it are constantly changing, so it is inevitable that some of the Internet addresses listed in this textbook will change.

Copyright © 2010, 2006, 2002, 1997 Pearson Education, Inc., publishing as Prentice Hall, Upper Saddle River, New Jersey 07458. All rights reserved. Manufactured in the United States of America. This publication is protected by Copyright, and permission should be obtained from the publisher prior to any prohibited reproduction, storage in a retrieval system, or transmission in any form or by any means, electronic, mechanical, photocopying, recording, or likewise. To obtain permission(s) to use material from this work, please submit a written request to Pearson Education, Inc., Permissions Department, 501 Boylston Street, Suite 900, Boston, MA 02116.

Library of Congress Cataloging-in-Publication Data

Robbins, Carolyn R.
  The job searcher's handbook / Carolyn R. Robbins.—4th ed.
    p. cm.
  Includes bibliographical references and index.
  ISBN-13: 978-0-13-235602-2
  ISBN-10: 0-13-235602-3
  1. Job hunting—United States—Handbooks, manuals, etc.   I. Title.
HF5382.75.U6R63 2010
650.140973—dc22

                                    2009005364

10 9 8 7 6 5 4 3 2 1

Prentice Hall
is an imprint of

www.pearsonhighered.com

ISBN 13: 978-0-13-235602-2
ISBN 10:   0-13-235602-3

Brief Contents

WITHDRAWN

WITHDRAWN

Contents

3 Organizing and Planning   84

Interviewing Made *Almost* Easy 110

Closing the Job Search Process 139

Appendix   158

Preface

We are now well into the 21st century, and with it comes more changes in the way employers are viewing prospective job applicants. Consequently, the methods used to job hunt are also changing. Since the first publication of *The Job Searcher's Handbook*, we have seen many changes in the world, in the job market, and the increase of a global workforce. We continue to see rapidly advancing and expanding technology and corporations that are struggling to be profitable in a roller-coaster economy. Beginning with the first edition, my objective has always been to provide people who are seeking employment with complete, up-to-date, and comprehensive instructions for being successful in that search. That objective has not changed with the writing of the second, third, and now fourth editions of this book.

To achieve this objective and to keep pace with job market trends, changes in the world of work, and the latest techniques and concepts, I have revised much of the material presented in the first, second, and third editions. I have also written and added one new chapter about closing the job search process and getting and keeping the job that takes job seekers one step further in knowing how to conduct themselves successfully and advance in the workplace. Since the publication of the previous editions, companies have continued to undergo many reorganizations. Major fluctuations in the job market have resulted from such alterations as corporate outsourcing, and economics have produced job-hunting retirees. Although the basic principles of job searching remain the same and the conventional methods are still valid, recent innovations do influence the ways in which people conduct a job search. The Internet and e-mail plus MySpace and YouTube websites have introduced new methods of communication so that a person seeking employment now has access to a wider range of exposure than ever before. Therefore, I have added information about new and exciting ways job seekers can use technology to market themselves to prospective employers.

During the past more than 25 years of teaching courses on job search skills and hiring guidelines for employers, counseling job seekers in my private practice, and placing people in jobs, I have consistently found that most people I encounter have no idea how to search for a job effectively. Often the information they do have is incorrect or obsolete. Consequently, from those experiences and the recognition of a need for guidelines that encompass the total job search process, I created *The Job Searcher's Handbook*.

Despite what many people believe, the job search does not begin with a resume. Rather it begins with discovering who you really are, what you want, and where you wish to go. Chapter 1, "Taking Inventory," leads you step by step through the process of discovering and clarifying your goals and values. It will also help you set your priorities, which must be established before you even begin to create a resume.

Chapter 2, "Documenting Yourself," will assist you in putting together the paperwork so necessary in today's competitive job market. Your resume, cover letter, portfolio, follow-up correspondence, and application forms must be impeccable to exceed the competition and convince prospective employers that you are someone they want to hire.

Once you have completed this preliminary preparation and analysis, the next critical phase of any job search, organizing and planning, is covered in Chapter 3, "Organizing and Planning." Devising an organized and well-thought-out plan is absolutely essential to avoid wasting time by moving in all the wrong directions. A plan that arranges each day with job leads, contacts, and interviews will also keep you from procrastinating.

Chapter 4, "Interviewing Made *Almost* Easy," has one major objective: to minimize fear and anxiety during interviewing. By knowing how interviews are conducted, what employers look for in applicants, and how you can fit into the current and future faces of the workplace, you can reduce your fear of interviewing. Now, in the 21st century as in the past, it is still very important that you be able to demonstrate to a prospective employer that you are capable of thinking strategically, can demonstrate versatility, and contribute to the company's goals. This is possible if you do the proper research before interviewing, and Chapter 4 shows you how. To maximize your opportunities and obtain job offers, do your research and use the techniques offered in this chapter.

The last chapter, "Closing the Job Search Process," covers the correct manner in which to close the interview, deal with rejection, and what to do between interviews. It follows with indispensable information on how to negotiate for the most equitable salary and benefit package. The chapter also offers advice on how to keep and advance in a job and be successful when you ask for a raise.

To all of my readers, I wish for you the old Latin saying, "Veni, vidi, vici" (I came, I saw, I conquered).

—*Carolyn R. Robbins*

To my friends: Jane Turk, Berni Ward, Ray Sumner, and Angie Hoegee who urged me to "go for it."

Special thanks go to my children, who have always given me encouragement and support in all of my pursuits: Doris Holloway, Pamela Gulbrandson, Hollis A.Gulbrandson, and Karyl Lynn Barnes.

Acknowledgments

My sincere thanks to all of the people who have been involved in the writing of all four editions of this book:

To those who reviewed this edition and offered constructive suggestions: Bruce Bloom, DeVry University–Chicago; Connie Egelman, Nassau Community College; Theresa Green Ervin, Indiana University–Bloomington; Eric Hoover, Virginia College; April Hudson, ITT Technical Institute; Margaret Kennedy, Lansing Community College; Lisa Kooperman, Marist College; and Edward Tucker, Lincoln College of Technology. To Carolyn Curtis of Naugatuck Valley Community College, Win Chesney of St. Louis Community College, and Susan Riley of DeVry University, for their expertise.

To the dean of Economic Development & Training and director of the Adult Short Classes, Tom Gorman, and the students at the North Platte Community College for their praise and encouragement. For Ann Melton, president of the Creative Unlimited Arts Council in North Platte, Nebraska, many thanks for introducing and recommending me to persons who would open new doors to my creating and teaching adult classes at the North Platte Community College and provide a market for *The Job Searcher's Handbook* at the A to Z Bookstore.

To my previous coworkers and employers, who gave me the highest of praise for my success in the placement of students in jobs and helped me develop the self-confidence that is needed for an endeavor such as this: Jerry Sirbu, owner of Platt College, Denver, Colorado, and Mike Schledorn, former owner of Denver Technical College and Director of the Denver Business College in Denver, Colorado.

Also in Denver, Colorado, to Angie Hoegee, director of General Education at Westwood College of Technology/North and instructor at Westwood/South for her editing and suggestions. To Ray Sumners, director and instructor of the bachelor programs for all campuses of Westwood College of Technology for his willingness to take the time out from his already overloaded schedule to create many exercises and graphics, and to share his knowledge for Chapters 1 and 5. To Jim Keefe, instructor and computer guru, and to Greg and Lynn Barnes, for their help whenever I needed assistance with the mechanics of computer operations. To Marija Oman Mohr, online instructor and coworker at Westwood/North, for her generosity in supplying me with articles and books with information on the Internet. To Rick Palmer, software test engineer and computer consultant, for all his technical assistance and feedback.

Special thanks to all the students and clients I've counseled and helped to find employment who have given me the highest of compliments and letters of reference over the past 25 years. A great deal of gratitude goes to Jane Turk, former human relations recruiter at Martin Marietta, and human resources manager for the City of Louisville, Colorado. Jane, who has been my friend, confidante, and contributor for many years, continues to supply me with forms and current information about the job-search process from an employer's point of view.

To Sande Johnson, executive editor at Pearson, and editorial assistant Lynda Cramer, for all their patience, wonderful expertise, and advice in the writing of this fourth edition.

Without all of the help and creativity from all these people, this book would not have been possible, and for this, I am forever grateful.

About the Author

"This book's step-by-step process for securing employment is superb! I found the author's style of writing down-to-earth, humorous, and extremely helpful."

Barry Shaffer, Computer Networking Instructor Westwood College of Technology, Denver, Colorado

"With Carolyn's help, I believe I would have gotten my job at Citicorp even without the course I took . . ."

Barry Kearns, Computer Programmer, Citicorp, Inc., Littleton, Colorado

"Carolyn Robbins was directly responsible for my getting the job I wanted with a great salary . . ."

Louis Baker, Computer Technician, Los Angeles

"I've read lots of career development books, and Ms. Robbins's is by far the best. The others gave you a lot of talk, but didn't really tell how to get your job . . ."

Valerie Wilson, Electronics Technician, Aurora, Colorado

"This author is excellent; she knows exactly what to do to get the job . . ."

Gary Hartman, Computer Programmer/Analyst, Boulder City, Utah

"Thank you for a wonderful class. It is one of the best I have ever taken."

Linda Woodward, Mid Plains Community College, North Platte, Nebraska

Carolyn Robbins is a private career consultant, instructor, seminar leader, and author who has been involved in the field of career development for more than 25 years. Acting as college job placement director/instructor, she consistently maintained 85 to 95 percent placement while providing career counseling and job placement in many technical and business fields throughout fluctuating economic periods. Robbins is a member of the University of Colorado at Denver Alumni, has served on the board, authored job search articles, and conducted workshops on resume writing, interviewing, and job leads. Robbins is also the author of an English composition textbook, *Beyond the Blank Page: Steps to Writing Well*. Robbins's widely used texts are known for their straightforward, succinct explanations and practical orientation.

Taking Inventory

A constructive approach to job searching, career
changing, or making any life-altering decision should
begin with self-evaluation. Steven Graber, author of
The Everything Get-a-Job Book, says, "One of the
biggest mistakes job seekers make is to start looking
for a job before they're really ready"[1]—and getting
ready begins with an honest self-assessment.

You can increase your chances of getting the job you want and being successful in it by taking the first step, that of honestly appraising who you are, what is important to you, and where you are going. You cannot honestly know what is going to make you happy and successful unless you first do some "inventorying." Therefore, contrary to popular belief, a job search does not begin with a resume; it begins with self-analysis.

Most people resist looking very long and hard at themselves. They are afraid to challenge their self-image and to examine their attitudes. They give very little thought to the context, the fundamentals of job searching, such as "What kind of person am I? What kind of people do I best interact with? Based on my values, what are the most important things I want in a job?" They usually just rationalize any self-evaluation away by saying, "Oh, I know me; I don't need all that stuff. I *know* what I want." However, when they begin to write their resume, they discover that they can't even construct a coherent job objective. In an interview, when asked what is most important to them, they mumble something about a good salary, good benefits, and so on. To avoid having this happen to you and to help you succeed in getting the job that is right for you, begin by examining three important areas: your values, attitudes, and goals.

Personal Values: How They Affect Job Choices

How do our values affect the choice of a job? Because you attribute your worth, merit, or usefulness to your values, they greatly influence career and job choices. Also, your values change. What was worthwhile to you in earlier jobs may not be that important now, and other things may be more important. So, if you want to make wise choices in job selection, clarifying your values and deciding what's really important to you is a necessary step. Completing this step will help you to be more focused in your job search and to make healthy decisions (without internal conflict) about which job offers to accept and which ones to reject. Steven Reiss, Ph.D., in his "Reiss Profile" agrees with this principle that "shared values produce team spirit and cohesiveness in the workplace, whereas conflicts of values lead to divisiveness and hidden agendas."[2]

When completing your self-analysis and deciding what is important to you, remember that self-evaluation is primarily a do-it-yourself project. Friends and family are not the ultimate authority on who you are or what you should do; *you* are the authority on you! Because their evaluation of you could be biased more toward their personal perception of you, is it may not be truly representative of what you believe is important. So, when deciding what's important to you, a useful exercise is to imagine you are on a island with no family or friends around you, and you have the choice of any job. What would be your choice of a job; what would you be doing?

Sadly, many people go to work each week hating Monday and praying for Friday, so to avoid that pitfall, it's vital that you take the time to assess your values and determine your needs in a job. From the list of personal values that follows, rate each one individually on a scale of 1 to 10, according to how important it is to you in the workplace. Do not *rank* them, that is, choosing only one as a "10," only one as a "9," and so on. They can be all 10s if that is how important they are to you. After you have rated them, go back and complete the statements after each value, and then write out how they relate to the job you are seeking. Ask yourself, "How does this value affect my choice of a job?" Describe in detail how and why each one is important.

PERSONAL VALUES

Rating scale: 1 = least important, 10 = most important

_____ 1. *Recognition:* "I feel the most recognized when an employer

_____

_____

_____

_____

_____ 2. *Independence:* "A supervisor monitoring what I do

_____

_____

_____

_____

_____ 3. *Challenge/Variety:* "I have to be challenged and have variety in my work or

_____

_____

_____

_____

_____ 4. *Money/Compensation:* "If I get paid (don't get paid) a salary that's equal to my worth, I

_____

_____

_____

_____

_____ 5. *Respect:* "I feel respected in my job when an employer

_____

_____

_____

_____

_____ 6. *Honesty:* "If my employer is dishonest, it does/doesn't affect me because

_____

_____

_____

_____

(continued)

PERSONAL VALUES Continued

_____ 7. *Personal Pride/Satisfaction:* "My personal pride and satisfaction with my job are derived from

_____

_____

_____

_____

_____ 8. *Health:* "My well-being and health are affected on the job

_____

_____

_____

_____

_____ 9. *Family:* "My family (those persons most important to me) comes first/second to my job because

_____

_____

_____

_____

_____ 10. *Education:* "It's important/not important that an employer assist me with furthering my education because

_____

_____

_____

_____

If other values of importance to you are not named on these pages, use the space provided to list them.

_____

_____

_____

_____

_____

_____

Based on how you rated your values and to get a clearer picture of where your priorities are, both personal and work related, go to the next few pages. There, you will build your *Personal Values Mountain* and plot your *Personal Values Wheel*.

Values Mountain

Values come in all shapes and colors. Some people divide values up into *Things & Processes, Intrapersonal* (things you value inside you), and *Interpersonal* (values between people).

Here are lists of some of those values. Over the next few pages, you will decide which of these values, or other values you add in, are the most important to you.

THINGS & PROCESSES

1. Prefer to work in *clean, orderly environment.*
2. Can tolerate *untidy workplace.*
3. Prefer *strict regulations.*
4. Prefer *low regulations.*
5. *Money/compensation.*
6. *Promotion or advancement.*
7. Prefer *casual wardrobe.*
8. Prefer *traditional wardrobe.*
9. *Slow-paced work* environment.
10. *Fast-paced work* environment.
11. *Task variety.*
12. *Similar tasks* every day.
13. *Like overtime,* more pay.
14. Prefer *time off,* no overtime.
15. *Flexible work schedules.*
16. *Fixed work schedule.*
17. Like to *travel.*
18. Do *not want to travel.*

INTRAPERSONAL VALUES

1. *Honesty* from boss/peers.
2. *Respect* from boss/peers.
3. Like to work with *details.*
4. Like to work with *big picture.*
5. Like to *take work home.*
6. *Leave work at work.*
7. Need to feel sense of *achievement.*
8. Would like a position with *power/status.*
9. Need to feel *personal pride and satisfaction.*
10. Want *recognition* for my work.
11. Like *autonomy,* no supervisor looking over my shoulder.
12. *Health.*
13. *Education and future training* opportunities.

INTERPERSONAL VALUES

1. Prefer to *work in teams.*
2. Prefer to *work alone.*
3. Like to *work directly with customers.*
4. Like to *work indirectly* to support customers.
5. Like to *communicate face to face* with others.
6. Prefer to *communicate with messages and e-mail.*
7. Like to *supervise others.*
8. *Don't want responsibility for others.*
9. *Family responsibility.*
10. *Child care.*
11. *Elder care.*

Personal Values Mountain

Look at this example of how to plot the things you value most on your *Values Mountain*. Then create your own *Values Mountain*. Place the most important thing on the top of the mountain, the second most important below that, and work your way down the mountain in descending order of priority of values.

Money & Compensation

Respect

Independence

Challenge and Variety in Work

Minimum Supervision

Clear Guidelines and Regulations

Casual Wardrobe

Fast-Paced Work

Time Off

Responsibility

Details

Team Decision Making

No Take-Home Work

Honesty

Family Responsibilities

Clean, Orderly Workplace

PERSONAL VALUES MOUNTAIN

List the things you value in your personal life and professional life. Consider the values listed on page 5. You can also add value items that are not in the previous lists. What is the most important thing in your life? Place it on the top line. What is the next most important thing you value? Place it on the second line from the top, and so on, until all the things you value are sorted down the mountain in descending importance.

Giving some thought to what is really important in your life will aid in your career choices. You can further clarify your values by completing a *Values Wheel.*

PERSONAL VALUES WHEEL

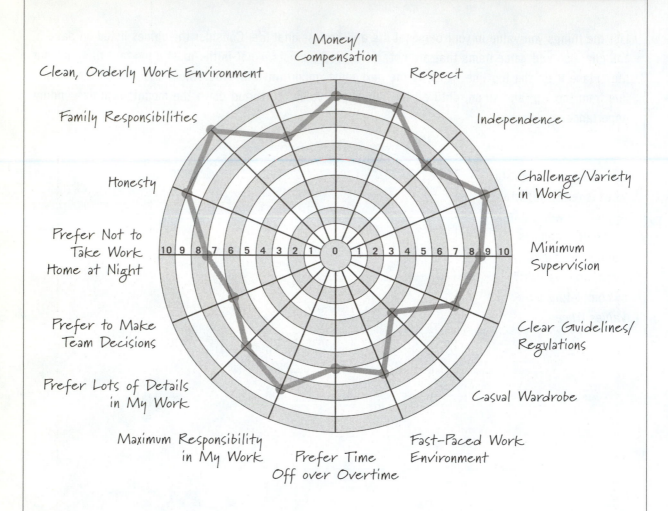

Write in the values you most care for (from your *Values Mountain*) on the outside of each of the spokes in your *Values Wheel*. Score each of these values from 0 to 10 based on how well you feel that value is now being met. Placing a dot on the 0 ring means that value is not being met at all. A dot on the 5 ring means you are satisfying that value about half of the time. A dot on the 10 ring means you are very satisfied, and it couldn't be better.

Connect the dots to form a graphic display of how well your values are currently being met. The short spokes of your graph indicate a desire for them to be better. When you begin your job search, you might ask yourself the question, "Will these values be better or worse at this new job?" This graph tells you what you are truly looking for in a career. Our productivity in the workplace is the greatest when many of our values are met.

PERSONAL VALUES WHEEL

Create your own *Personal Values Wheel.*

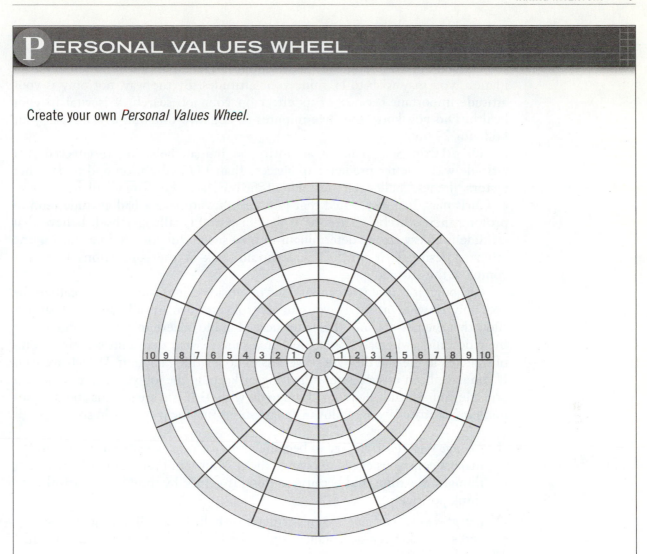

Attitude

What exactly is meant by attitude? How do you define it? Webster's definition is that an **attitude** is "a manner, disposition, feeling, position, etc. toward a person or thing." The relationship between your values and your attitude is that a value, an idea, or belief you hold to be true arouses an emotional response. That emotional response creates an attitude either for or against certain things. For example, if you value exercise and believe it is the only way to be healthy, your attitude toward those who exercise will be that they are healthy and those who do not are unhealthy. Obviously, this could be a faulty assumption based simply on your attitude; therefore, it is wise to examine the attitudes you've acquired. Is it possible that they are based on some faulty thinking?

Because you began to acquire your attitudes as a child and have continued to add to them throughout your life, they are deeply ingrained, and you may not even be aware of how they are affecting your life and your career. What is your attitude most of the time? Positive or negative? Do you believe good things are ahead for you? Or do you think, "Oh, this is too good to be true; I just know it can't last." If you find that your general outlook on life is one of doubt and trepidation, you may wish to examine your attitudes. By the way, not only is your attitude important because of its effect on your job search, it is vital to your health. Did you know that five minutes of negative thinking discourages your body for 24 hours?

Dr. Martin Seligman, an authority on human behavior, discovered that attitude was a better predictor of success than I.Q., education and most other factors.[3] James Challenger, president of the outplacement firm Challenger, Gray, & Christmas, Inc., has stated that job seekers who have a bad attitude tend to prolong their search. Therefore, if Seligman and Challenger both believe that attitude is a very strong determinant in how successful you are in acquiring the job you desire, is it possible you should look at the suggestions here and complete the attitude quiz?

Although it is true you cannot control outside things such as the weather, the economy, or what others do, you can control your own attitude. Research studies show that the persons most likely to succeed in life believe they have control over their destinies, whereas "losers" feel that luck is what determines their accomplishments in life and they are powerless to do anything about it. Which are you? If you have been unsuccessful in getting or keeping the job you really want, is it possible your attitude had something to do with it? If you are serious about examining inner attitudes, the following suggestions may help you to do so.

1. *Change your thinking.* Try to become aware of your negative attitudes and make a conscious effort to change them. Your mind can hold only one thought at a time, and because nothing is gained by thinking negatively, think positively.

2. *Accept yourself and others* Don't criticize or belittle; we all have weaknesses and strengths. Self-acceptance comes first. Until you master that, you will not be able to accept others.

3. Above all, *believe that good things do happen* and there is an abundance of everything you desire. Remember, it's your choice. You can remain a slave to negative attitudes that limit your ability to take advantage of the wonderful opportunities and jobs waiting for you, or you can decide now to begin thinking positive thoughts and doing positive actions.

4. Keep this thought in mind: *It is our attitude toward life that determines life's attitude toward us.*

To determine what your attitude is today, take the following attitude quiz.

HOW'S YOUR ATTITUDE?

To discover what kind of attitude you have at present, answer the 15 questions here as *honestly* as possible, using the following scoring system:

Heartily Agree	Agree	Neutral	Slightly Disagree	Disagree
5	4	3	2	1

_____ 1. I take time to admire flowers or something pretty both at work and at home.

_____ 2. I think my fortunes will increase and life will be much better for me next year.

_____ 3. I hate to work closely with people; I prefer to work alone and be responsible for my own work.

_____ 4. I think the mores, values, and work ethics of this nation are deteriorating quickly.

_____ 5. Employers look for people not only for their skills but also for their ability to deal effectively with others and contribute to the company's growth.

_____ 6. I have the right to hold a grudge against people who have wronged me.

_____ 7. I believe it is a waste of time to set goals because things change so fast, it doesn't do any good to set them.

_____ 8. When there are abrupt changes at work, I freely support them and look for ways to take advantage of these changes.

_____ 9. It really isn't important whether I get along with others because I'm really good at what I do.

_____ 10. When someone informs me that I have made an error or done something wrong, I know they are just trying to put me down and build themselves up.

_____ 11. I frequently compliment and recognize my peers for the good work they do.

_____ 12. A wise person admits to mistakes.

_____ 13. When I think back on my life, I see more mistakes and failures than I see successes.

_____ 14. The way in which I think about my job makes me very productive.

_____ 15. If I have had a lot of problems in previous jobs, it was because people just didn't understand me.

Scoring: Reverse-score questions 3, 4, 6, 7, 9, 10, 13, and 15 as shown here:

Heartily Agree	=	1
Agree	=	2
Neutral	=	3
Slightly Disagree	=	4
Disagree	=	5

(continued)

HOW'S YOUR ATTITUDE? Continued

For the remaining questions (1, 2, 5, 8, 11, 12, and 14), give them the point value according to the scoring table at the beginning of this exercise. Total your points.

If you scored . . .

65 or over	Great attitude!
60–64	Excellent attitude. Very positive thinker!
55–59	Good attitude. Your thinking is somewhat positive.
50–54	Fair; you are half and half. Sometimes your attitude is good, but sometimes it isn't up to par.
49 and below	Don't send out your resume until you have practiced positive thinking.

If you scored 49 or below, ask yourself, "Is this the kind of attitude that will help me to get the job I want and to keep it?" Probably not! Reread the previous page, and then begin to practice the four suggestions for positive thinking.

Interests, Wants, and Needs

During the job search, you will need to create a resume and be able to sell yourself to employers by describing who you are and what you can do for them. You also need to know what you want so you can make the correct decision about which job is right for you. If you can't identify what you truly want, you will probably settle for what you *think is possible* rather than what you *truthfully desire*. The following exercises will help you prepare for these decisions.

For additional assistance in assessing your career interests, go to the website www.ZDNet.com and click on "2007 IT Salary and Skills Survey." This site will give you a link to one of popular interest, the "Campbell Interest and Skill Survey." For $18 plus tax, you can take a career self-assessment (CISS) written by David Campbell, Ph.D., and view the report. Another popular site that many teachers and career counselors use is the Myers-Briggs Career Test. Key in Myers-Briggs Career Test Online, and click on the link "Free Career Test." You will learn what the 24 most popular careers and the 10 least popular ones are for your type. This program also explores how 16 different personality types fit with the tasks needed to perform in many professional occupations. Another tried and proven online testing program, the self-scoring Strong Interest Explorer, is accessible by keying in www.psychometrics.com. This test measures interests in a broad range of occupations and work and leisure activities, as well as how they are similar to the interests of people successfully employed in a wide range of occupations. The test cost is $45 for a package of 10 or $7.50 each.

WHAT DO I WANT?

For each list, rank the items according to how important they are to you, using a scale of 1 to 10, with 1 the least important and 10 the most important.

What Do I Want for Myself? (your own personal wants and needs)

____ 1. Popularity

____ 2. Wealth

____ 3. Nice figure, physique

____ 4. Good friends

____ 5. Reputation as a good person, intellectual, and hard worker

____ 6. Honors, awards, recognition

____ 7. One special person in my life

____ 8. Privacy

____ 9. A family

____ 10. Good health

What Do I Want from My Job/Career? (aim for the most nearly ideal)

____ 1. Status, position

____ 2. First-rate salary

____ 3. Personal satisfaction

____ 4. Friendly coworkers

____ 5. Fair, equitable boss

____ 6. Nice office, work environment

____ 7. Responsibility, challenge

____ 8. Variety

____ 9. Opportunity to advance

____ 10. Top benefits package

What Do I Want for My Future? (5, 10, or 15 years from now)

____ 1. Further education, training

____ 2. New activities, interests to pursue

____ 3. Personal and emotional growth

____ 4. The highest position in my field

____ 5. Retirement/semiretirement to do the things listed in numbers 6 through 10

____ 6. A nice, modern home

____ 7. Money to travel, explore

____ 8. All the latest tech gadgets

____ 9. An expensive late-model car

____ 10. Good health

What Do I Like to Do in My Leisure Time? (some of these also relate to the workplace)

____ 1. Watch TV

____ 2. Sports, as a participant

____ 3. Write poetry, stories

____ 4. Play computer games

____ 5. Do crafts, artwork

____ 6. Read

____ 7. Go to movies

____ 8. Travel, camping

____ 9. Try new things

____ 10. Sleep

PRIORITIES CHART

Select your top five personal desires and top five professional desires. They can be from any of the four areas, and some may even overlap from personal into professional and vice versa. Award them the same points as you did on the previous page. Your scores should give you a good idea of where your top priorities lie and give you a direction as to what kinds of companies and positions you should look for that would offer you the kind of personal and professional environment you need to be successful and happy. What do your totals tell you?

PERSONAL	POINTS
1. _____	_____
2. _____	_____
3. _____	_____
4. _____	_____
5. _____	_____
Total	_____

PROFESSIONAL	POINTS
1. _____	_____
2. _____	_____
3. _____	_____
4. _____	_____
5. _____	_____
Total	_____

W HO AM I?

Answer the following questions to discover the things you honestly enjoy and those that you are especially good at.

1. In all areas of my life, what things do I do really well? In what areas am I most competent?

_____

_____

_____

_____

2. At this time, what is the highest position in my field for which I believe I could qualify?

_____

_____

_____

_____

3. What things am I doing now or have I done in the past that were the most enjoyable or rewarding to me? (These do not have to be job related; they can be from any area of your life.)

_____

_____

_____

_____

4. If I had an Aladdin's lamp and had three wishes, who would I be, what would I be doing, and with whom would I be doing it? (Have some fun with this; who knows, dreams do come true!)

_____

_____

_____

_____

5. What are the things that people most often compliment me on?

_____

_____

_____

_____

(continued)

WHO AM I? Continued

6. In my opinion, what has been my greatest accomplishment? What abilities, both technical and personal, do I possess that enabled me to accomplish it? (List all the abilities you can think of, because you're going to use these in an exercise later.)

   _____

   _____

   _____

   _____

7. Using the space provided or a separate piece of paper, imagine your ideal day and write it out in complete and vivid detail. Describe colors, places, feelings, exact amounts, and so on. Let your imagination run free; don't let your doubts about what is possible get in the way. Think about it: Everything that exists today once began as an idea in someone's mind. All our modern technology in business, in the home, and in entertainment came from someone who believed there was a better way to live. Who's to say that what you imagine can't become a reality?

   _____

   _____

   _____

   _____

   _____

   _____

   _____

   _____

   _____

   _____

INVENTORYING YOUR STRENGTHS

Mark an X beside those strengths that describe you as you are now. Then circle the 10 that are *most like you*. When you finish, you will have a list of specific items for selling yourself on paper and in the interview, and also for completing the *Skills and Abilities Wheel* later in the chapter.

Academic	Courageous	Honest	Outgoing	Sincere
Accurate	Creative	Humorous	Painstaking	Sociable
Active	Curious	Idealistic	Patient	Spontaneous
Adaptable	Daring	Imaginative	Peaceable	Spunky
Adventurous	Deliberate	Independent	Persevering	Stable
Affectionate	Democratic	Individualized	Pleasant	Steady
Aggressive	Dependable	Industrious	Poised	Strong
Alert	Determined	Informal	Polite	Strong-minded
Ambitious	Dignified	Ingenious	Practical	Sympathetic
Artistic	Discreet	Intellectual	Precise	Tactful
Assertive	Dominant	Intelligent	Progressive	Teachable
Attractive	Eager	Inventive	Prudent	Tenacious
Bold	Easygoing	Kind	Purposeful	Thorough
Broad-minded	Efficient	Leisurely	Quick	Thoughtful
Businesslike	Emotional	Lighthearted	Quiet	Tolerant
Calm	Energetic	Likable	Rational	Tough
Capable	Enterprising	Logical	Realistic	Trusting
Careful	Enthusiastic	Loyal	Reasonable	Trustworthy
Cautious	Fair-minded	Mature	Reflective	Unaffected
Charming	Farsighted	Methodical	Relaxed	Unassuming
Cheerful	Firm	Meticulous	Reliable	Understanding
Clear thinking	Flexible	Mild	Reserved	Unexcitable
Clever	Forceful	Moderate	Resourceful	Uninhibited
Competent	Formal	Modest	Responsible	Verbal
Competitive	Frank	Natural	Retiring	Versatile
Confident	Friendly	Obliging	Robust	Warm
Conscientious	Generous	Open-minded	Self-confident	Wholesome
Conservative	Gentle	Opportunistic	Sensible	Wise
Considerate	Good-natured	Optimistic	Sensitive	Witty
Cool	Healthy	Organized	Serious	Zany
Cooperative	Helpful	Original	Sharp-witted	

SKILLS AND ABILITIES ASSESSMENT

This is an opportunity for you to assess all your abilities, your marketable skills (technical, educational, personal), and your achievements. Don't leave anything out; even though you might believe it isn't significant, you may discover an employer who is looking for that particular skill, ability, or expertise.

1. List all your personal qualities and characteristics, such as dependability, enthusiasm, honesty, high energy level, tact, cooperativeness, punctuality, and sense of humor.

_____

_____

_____

_____

2. List all your marketable skills that are work related, such as leadership, ability to learn quickly and retain what you learn, effectiveness at prioritizing, innovation, and investigative and problem-solving skills.

_____

_____

_____

_____

3. List your vocational and educational skills. Examples: computer programming and networking; computer maintenance and repair; information technology auditor, search engine optimizer; service-related skills such as hospitality, medical, and accounting; and mechanical or drawing skills.

_____

_____

_____

_____

4. List all your accomplishments: personal, educational, and job related. A high grade point average (GPA), scholarships earned, honors, improvements in the workplace that you've created, promotions, volunteer work, and community service are all achievements that can sell an employer on your value to them and help you net a job offer.

_____

_____

_____

_____

SKILLS AND ABILITIES WHEEL

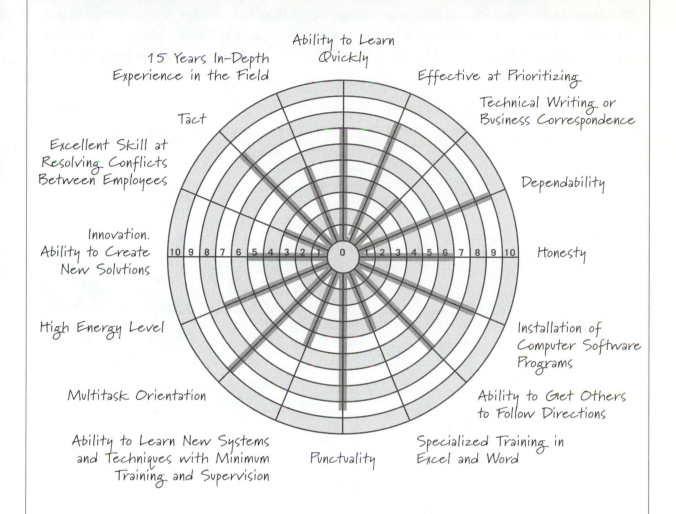

A skill is something you do well. An ability is the power to do something without necessarily having the skills to do it. In the job search process, you must have a clear idea of what skills and abilities you have to offer an employer. Review the *Inventorying Your Strengths* exercise as well as the *Skills and Abilities Assessment,* and decide which of them to place on your wheel.

Although we all have skill sets and abilities, not all of them are at their peak. Pick the skills and abilities you feel you possess and place them on the spokes of your *Skills and Abilities Wheel*. Rate your skills and abilities on a 0 to 10 scale. Of course, 0 means you are not capable of performing that skill without constant supervision or have no ability in this area but are willing to learn. A score of 5 means you could do the job half the time or have a 50 percent chance of success if given an opportunity. A score of 10 means you feel confident to apply that skill with minimum or no supervision or feel confident that given an opportunity, your abilities would almost guarantee you success.

See the nearby example. The short spokes are the areas that could be improved in the future to make yourself more marketable. The long spokes represent what you can sell immediately.

SKILLS AND ABILITIES WHEEL

The completed *Skills and Abilities Wheel* is your sales program in an interview. The long spokes will be your first features to sell an employer. The next longest spokes will be sold as additional skills and abilities that can be brought up to speed with brief training. The lowest spokes are areas you would like to improve to be more competitive.

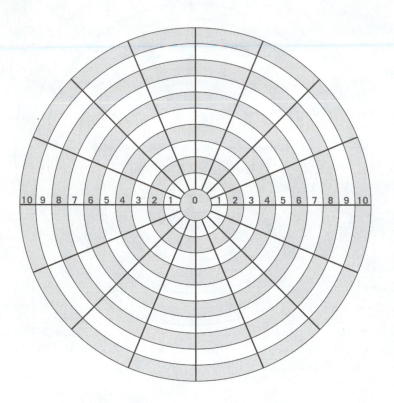

Success Through Goal Setting

Now that you've taken the steps to inventory your interests, needs, and wants, and have defined your strengths, skills, and abilities, you're ready for the final step to finalize your package for success. Success often begins with a commitment to self-improvement through goal setting. It's remarkable how few persons are aware of this, and they live their lives tolerating situations that are not to their liking rather than being motivated to change them. Little do they realize that goal setting is the way to make all things possible. Setting goals will give you the pattern for opportunity, add aim to your energy, focus your talents, and even structure your time.

Inside every successful person, you will find an avid goal setter. In a study at Yale University, 20 questions were asked of graduating seniors. Three had to do with goals: Have you set goals? Have you written them down? Do you have a plan to accomplish them? Only 3 percent answered yes to those three questions. Twenty years later, surviving members of that class participated in another study. The 3 percent who had said yes to goals were more happily married, more successful, had a better family life, and enjoyed better health than their non-goal-oriented classmates.

If you want to be successful and acquire those things you selected on the previous pages as your priorities, defining your goals and making a written plan for achieving them is absolutely necessary. Why do they have to be written? you ask. Well, at any given moment, you can be consciously aware of only about 30 to 40 percent of what's in your mind. If your goals are only "in your head," they are likely to stay there! You can stay focused and organized only by writing your goals out. Otherwise, you get hung up in day-to-day frustrations and problems, and you run the risk of missing out on opportunities that come your way.

Guidelines for Setting Goals

The basic principles and techniques for setting and achieving your goals are actually quite simple. Maybe that's why so many people don't do it; they are looking for something that is tedious and difficult. Is it possible that we believe if something comes easily, it probably isn't worth much? This is not always true.

When setting your goals, keep in mind that you need to set short-term goals: those you want to acquire in, say, a month to six months or maybe even in a week. These are followed by long-term goals, things you want to happen in one, three, or five years, maybe longer. If you set only long-term goals, your focus is too far in the future; you need a plan that will break those long-term goals down into more manageable blocks of time. For example, your long-term goal might be to be employed with the company of your choice making a top-notch salary and on your way to an excellent promotion. How exactly are you going to obtain that long-term goal? You must set short-term goals to reach in the interim. What *specifically* are you going to do to get that job? Obviously, your first short-term goal would be to do some research to find out just where that kind of job exists. What skills and abilities does it require? Your immediate goal might be to learn where this information could be found. You could begin with MSN Careers, CareerBuilder.com, for excellent information on jobs that are currently available and descriptions/salaries of those jobs. The second short-term goal would be to assess your skills and abilities to determine if you qualify for that kind of position. As you can see, many short-term goals need to be set and achieved before you can work on the long-term goal. The more you break your long-term goals down into smaller tasks and increments of time, the more successful you'll be in obtaining them.

A good goal statement should answer the three following questions:

1. *What* is going to happen?
2. *When* is it going to happen?
3. *How* is it going to happen?

Here are seven basic steps to assist you in setting well-defined, specific, and clearly stated goals:

1. *State your goal specifically and completely so you know exactly what it is that you desire.* The more detailed your goal statement, the better you will be able to

visualize yourself actually having or doing what it is that you want. It's a fact: Most people spend more time planning their vacations than they do planning their careers or their lives. You must plan for your future; you have to live there!

2. *Set dates for your short-term and long-term goals.* Even if they have to be revised later, setting them will keep you from the "plague of procrastination." Caution: Don't let yourself get caught in a trap of feeling that you're a failure if you don't make those deadlines! If you miss a goal, simply evaluate where you are at the time and set new dates. You can't always know what is going to happen in the future.

3. *Goals should be realistic and reachable, but don't be afraid to strive for something that seems a bit out of reach.* If you are really determined and really want this goal, then set preliminary, short-term goals. Assess your lack of knowledge or expertise, and then plan a method for acquiring any skills you lack. On one hand, goals set too low are not really goals at all; they don't motivate you and could be a sign you are insecure, that you're "playing it safe." On the other hand, goals that are too high or unrealistic can destroy your enthusiasm and self-confidence when you fail to achieve them. Above all, don't give up if you don't succeed on your first attempt. How many attempts did it take you to learn to ride a bike, drive a car, or program your computer? Did you give up after the first or second try?

4. *Goals must be measurable.* This is why you set short-term goals. How will you know where you are in terms of acquiring your long-term goal if you don't set benchmarks or yardsticks to measure your progress toward that ultimate goal? For instance, if your long-term goal is to get a job in six months, the one you've dreamed of and worked hard toward acquiring the skills for, what would be the first thing you must do? What would you need to do this week, next week, and so on? Let's say that you know you must market your resume to at least 20 to 30 firms before getting an interview, and the interviewing process can take up to several weeks or a few months. What do you think your time frame for your short-term goals would be to get that job in six months?

5. *Make certain your goals are your very own goals, not things someone else wants for you.* If a goal is not yours, you won't be committed to it. All too often, parents, spouses, lovers, and those you admire exert an unknowing influence over your choices in life. Setting goals to please *them* won't work.

6. *Have fun!* As the bumper sticker reads, "Life is a game to be played, not a puzzle to be solved." To keep a balance in your life and take setbacks with a positive attitude, you need to have a good sense of humor. People will want to be around you if you're pleasant and enjoyable. Also, if attaining your goals means "all work and no play," you may feel overwhelmed and give up.

7. *It's critical that you identify your internal roadblocks, self-imposed barriers that could cause you to self-sabotage no matter how good your plans are.* The most damaging roadblock is usually right between your ears; it's that thought, that belief you're not good enough, not capable of accomplishing your goals. You know, the little voice in your head that says, "Who do I think I'm kidding, I'll never make it; there's probably someone else who knows more or does it better than I." I've found that in the majority of my students' goal-setting worksheets, they repeatedly express the idea that they are afraid they are not "good enough" to acquire the job goal they described in number 1. Recognize that the internal messages of

"I'm not good enough," "He or she is better, smarter, than I" stem from an earlier period in your life when some uncaring or unthinking person might have been attempting to control you. *These messages are no longer relevant; get rid of them!* Many excellent books currently on the market are designed to help you achieve a healthy sense of self-esteem and promote a comfortable confidence in your abilities. Two that I've found to be inspiring are *You'll See It When You Believe It* by Wayne Dyer and *Psychology of Success: Finding Meaning in Work and Life* by Denis Waitley.

Begin today to move in the direction you want to go. First, review the two sample goal-setting worksheets on the following pages. Then, using the blank worksheet on pages 28–29, set your goals for three to six months or a year from now and design plans to achieve them. As a goal-directed person, you will find many doors open for you that otherwise would have been closed. Once you have your goals written out and your plan in place, start visualizing them as already being accomplished. Don't minimize the power of visualization; major athletes, sports teams, and winners from all walks of life use it. Visualizing leads to desire, and desire leads to action and belief. You can't hit a target that you can't see! If possible, cut out pictures of what you desire and put them where you'll see them daily. This will help embed them in your mind and remind you of where you are going. It's also a wonderful cure for procrastination. "It's been proven that an idea, a dream that is consciously and persistently held in the mind, will manifest itself into reality," according to Henry David Thoreau.

One final thought from author Rudyard Kipling: "If you don't get what you want, it's either a sign that you didn't seriously want it or that you tried to bargain over the price."

GOAL SETTING (SAMPLE)

1. I believe setting goals is important because:

   goals are the road map to your future. They are the motivation behind actions. Without goals, life can be rather aimless and without direction. Direction = accomplishment.

2. My *immediate* job goal (the one I'm seeking now) is (include *specific* details on salary, type of company, location, and any important particulars about the job you plan to attain. The more specific your details, the more easily you can visualize them):

   one that will lend me the opportunity to develop skills that I can use as a foundation for a better job. I will make no less than $15 an hour with a computer firm in Houston, Texas.

3. The main benefits and rewards (both internal and external) that I will receive from reaching this goal are:

   (1) transferable job skills, (2) gaining experience in my field to move up in the company, and (3) the satisfaction that I have accomplished what I planned upon graduation.

4. The roadblocks (internal: faulty thinking, assumptions, etc., and external: lack of skills, training, etc.) that I need to remove to reach my goal are:

   (1) fatigue from juggling an already full schedule, (2) thinking I am not good enough, and (3) believing that people with more experience are the ones who get the jobs.

5. Actions I am going to take to get rid of these roadblocks are:

   (1) planning my time more efficiently so I can get the rest I need, (2) delegating external responsibilities to my husband and other family members, and (3) reminding myself every day that I do have the skills needed to get this immediate job and I have other qualities that employers look for, such as a good attitude, willingness to learn, and flexibility.

6. The skills and knowledge I need to reach my goal (those I have now and those I need to acquire) are:

   (1) the technical knowledge and skills that I'm now learning in college, (2) good time management, and (3) how to sell myself to an employer.

(continued)

GOAL SETTING (SAMPLE) Continued

7. Individuals, clubs, organizations, and groups that will help me attain my job goal are:

   (1) my husband and family, (2) my teachers, (3) the trade organizations for computer networking, and (4) most of all, myself, by following the steps outlined in this book and advice from others in the field.

8. My action plan (the *specific steps* that I must take to reach the immediate job goal I described in statement 2) is:

   A. *make out a time-management schedule for work and to meet the needs of my family and children*

   B. *continue to maintain my current positive attitude and GPA*

   C. *create an honest and impeccable resume and cover letter*

   D. *conduct several informational interviews to prepare myself better for interviewing*

   E. *complete the necessary follow-up on leads, interviews, and so on.*

   F.

   G.

I promise myself that I will follow the steps I've just outlined, visualize myself as already in possession of my goal, and do everything in my power to obtain this goal.

Today's date:

Date for the completion of my goal:

My signature:

After you've completed this form for your immediate job goal, you can use this same outline for writing your personal, financial, or spiritual goals.

GOAL SETTING (SAMPLE)

1. I believe setting goals is important because:

   having goals gives you something to strive for, something to motivate you. If you don't set goals for what you want, you have very little control over your life and what you get; you will probably just take whatever comes along.

2. My *immediate* job goal (the one I'm seeking now) is (include *specific* details on salary, type of company, location, and any important particulars about the job you plan to attain. The more specific your details, the more easily you can visualize them):

   securing a position in the computer networking field with a small to medium-size company, one that is progressive and stable. It will be located in the north metro area, and I will be earning a beginning salary of approximately $35,000 a year. Most importantly, I will be happy to go to work every day doing what I enjoy and will not consider it a job.

3. The main benefits and rewards (both internal and external) that I will receive from reaching this goal are:

   I will have a good budget plan and be able to pay my bills plus have money left over to enjoy my life. I will feel good about myself and what I do. Also, I will gain valuable experience so that I can move on to bigger and better things in a few years.

4. The roadblocks (internal: faulty thinking, assumptions, etc., and external: lack of skills, training, etc.) that I need to remove to reach my goal are:

   I don't give myself much credit for my experience and knowledge, and thinking that maybe the job market is not so good out there. I really don't have any external roadblocks except maybe some negative people who I think are my friends.

5. Actions I am going to take to get rid of these roadblocks are:

   I will keep telling myself that I do know my stuff, and I'm proving it every day at school. Even if an ad says they want "X" number of years of experience, I will apply for it and prove to them that I am capable of doing what the position requires. I will also try to choose my friends very carefully so that I am not around negative people.

6. The skills and knowledge I need to reach my goal (those I have now and those I need to acquire) are:

   the skills I'm learning now, the ones I've acquired from previous jobs such as good work ethics, team playing, and my exceptional ability to stay motivated, determined, and willing to get the job done correctly and on time.

(continued)

GOAL SETTING (SAMPLE) Continued

7. Individuals, clubs, organizations, and groups that will help me attain my job goal are:

   (1) the Career Development Department here at the college, (2) my reference people, whom I will keep in close touch with, (3) my teachers and people I know who are already in the field, and (4) trade organizations and publications related to my field.

8. My action plan (the *specific steps* that I must take to reach the immediate job goal I described in statement 2) is:

   A. I will graduate from college. I need to keep this vision clear; just because I'm almost finished doesn't mean I can slack off now.

   B. I will prepare my resume and cover letters carefully and honestly so that they will assist me in securing interviews.

   C. I will visit with the job placement personnel here and follow up on leads they give me.

   D. I will keep in close touch with them, especially after I graduate.

   E. I will post my resume and cover letter on the Internet and circulate them to let companies know I'm available and what I can offer them.

   F. I will go to all interviews and present myself positively and professionally in order to get job offers.

   G. I will do the proper follow-up on all leads, calls, and interviews.

I promise myself that I will follow the steps I've just outlined, visualize myself as already in possession of my goal, and do everything in my power to obtain this goal.

Today's date:

Date for the completion of my goal:

My signature:

After you've completed this form for your immediate job goal, you can use this same outline for writing your personal, financial, or spiritual goals.

GOAL SETTING

1. I believe setting goals is important because:

_____

_____

_____

2. My *immediate* job goal (the one I'm seeking now) is (include *specific* details on salary, type of company, location, and any important particulars about the job you plan to attain. The more specific your details, the more easily you can visualize them):

_____

_____

_____

3. The main benefits and rewards (both internal and external) that I will receive from reaching this goal are:

_____

_____

_____

4. The roadblocks (internal: faulty thinking, assumptions, etc., and external: lack of skills, training, etc.) that I need to remove to reach my goal are:

_____

_____

_____

5. Actions I am going to take to get rid of these roadblocks are:

_____

_____

_____

_____

6. The skills and knowledge I need to reach my goal (those I have now and those I need to acquire) are:

_____

_____

(continued)

GOAL SETTING (SAMPLE) Continued

7. Individuals, clubs, organizations, and groups that will help me attain my job goal are:

_____

_____

_____

8. My action plan (the *specific steps* that I must take to reach the immediate job goal I described in statement 2) is:

A. _____

_____

B. _____

_____

C. _____

_____

D. _____

_____

E. _____

_____

F. _____

_____

G. _____

_____

I promise myself that I will follow the steps I've just outlined, visualize myself as already in possession of my goal, and do everything in my power to obtain this goal.

Today's date: _____

Date for the completion of my goal: _____

My signature: _____

After you've completed this form for your immediate job goal, you can use this same outline for writing your personal, financial, or spiritual goals.

NOTES

1. Steven Graber, *The Everything Get-a-Job Book* (Avon, MA: Adams Media, 2000).

2. Steven Reiss, "Reiss Profile of Fundamental Goals and Motivational Sensitivities." Available at www.reissprofile.com.

3. Martin Seligman, Wikipedia, the free encyclopedia, April 10, 2008.

Documenting Yourself

A job search, to a large extent, is made by preparing paperwork. In any employment market, whether there's an abundance or scarcity of jobs, it is imperative that you prepare your paperwork carefully so that you do not get eliminated in the first round. It is highly unlikely that you can get a job just by visiting a few employers and having two or three brief interviews. A manager for professional recruiting and university relations at General Electric remarked that when companies are presented with candidates for a position, they all look for differences among applicants to separate the best from the rest. The first screening that occurs is based on the paperwork.

Employers, even in small to mid-size companies, usually receive 200 or more resumes each week, and very few of those have been proofread for basic spelling and grammar mistakes. Job seekers include either too much or too little information. That's why most of them end up in file 13—in other words, the waste paper basket. They usually are not read and then discarded. If the person applying for the company's opening doesn't take the time to prepare a quality, well-written resume, why should employers waste their time reading it?

Now more than ever, employers are requiring both resumes *and* cover letters. Ninety-five percent of all employment hires begin with the resume. Companies use your paperwork as a screening device to weed out the unqualified, and often just to get the stack down to a manageable level so that they can get on with the interviewing and get someone on board. If you don't include a cover letter, that alone could disqualify you if the response to an opening is high.

Five documents are required for your job search:

1. The *resume*, to help you get interviews.
2. The *cover letter*, which not only reinforces what is on the resume but also gives you the opportunity to sell yourself to the employer.
3. The *application form*, which, if not properly completed, could prevent you from getting the job.
4. *Follow-up correspondence*, the thank-you and no-thank-you letters sent after interviews and job offers.
5. *Your portfolio*, which gives the employer a complete accounting of what you have to offer—your education, you experience, your skills, and your achievements.

The instructions on the following pages will give you some simple techniques for writing a sound, results-getting resume and cover letter, show you how to complete the application forms correctly, and provide you with samples and suggestions for follow-up correspondence. Instructions on how to build your portfolio are provided in Chapter 4, "Interviewing Made *Almost* Easy."

Writing an effective resume and cover letter need not be painful. Look at the process as an opportunity to present yourself as a positive, willing, and motivated person who can be an asset to the company of your choice. Creating a positive and personalized tool for marketing yourself to prospective employers can actually be an uplifting experience.

Resume Preparation

The major purpose of the resume is to help you to get interviews. If it does that, it has done its job. If your preparation is substandard and your resume is poorly written, this will diminish your chances of getting interviews and, subsequently, a job. Remember, your resume is your first introduction to the employer; therefore, you must be extremely careful to present your qualifications in the most positive and professional manner. If your resume doesn't pass this initial inspection, you will be stuck on first base, wondering why you aren't being called for interviews.

Gathering Information

To begin creating a convincing resume, first gather all your background information and compile it on the blank worksheets provided for you in this chapter. If you already have a fairly recent resume, you can use that as a worksheet, and then revise and update your material. Don't worry about organization at this point; just get all the information down so you have a complete record of your background and qualifications. You'll organize it later. Be sure you include everything you have done, been a part of, attended, and so on. Many people overlook vital information at this stage, believing it not to be important. Trust me, the item you leave out just might be the one thing an employer is looking for.

Organizing Your Information

Once you have your background information down on paper, the next step is to organize it. At this point, you want to decide what you are going to include based on the job you are targeting. As you organize your information, keep in mind that your resume is not an obituary; nor is it your life history. Separate your jobs into fragments and explain them. For example, don't say that your job title was "office help" or "accountant" and stop there. Divide the job into such functions as telephone sales, inventory, computer application training, and written communications. Be sure to describe each job in terms of accomplishments and results. Many resumes are discarded because they include too much data, so concentrate on using only relevant information that will interest the employers in your field and encourage them to call you for an interview. Many employers, myself included, have received hundreds of resumes where the applicants just rambled on and on with a total disregard for any pertinence to the position for which they were applying. These are the resumes that get rejected, the ones that are called "pink slip" resumes. Unfortunately, they are so common that Robert Half, head of Robert Half International, a San Francisco–based employment firm, has written a book compiling the many resume blunders he has encountered over the years. Keep in mind that human resources directors tell me they receive 25 to 100 or more resumes each week and of those, only 5 percent lead to an interview.

When you have decided on the material to include, you are ready to choose a format or design. The manner in which you present your information is as important as what you say because it is perceived as part of your professional image. The format you choose should introduce you to an employer in the most favorable light. The following descriptions and the examples in this chapter and in the appendix will help you decide on the style that is best for your individual needs and the job or career you are targeting. Whether you intend to mail, e-mail, or hand-deliver your resume also has a bearing on how you format it.

Resume Styles

he two basic styles of resumes are the *chronological* and the *functional* formats. All others are variations of these two.

Chronological Format

A **chronological resume** (see Exhibit 2.1) lists your jobs, education, and events in a chronological order. Items are presented backward, beginning with your present job or school and working back in time. The chronological resume is probably the most common and the easiest to write. It is generally used when you have a very stable and impressive work background with no major job gaps. One of its advantages is that it enables you to show progression and increasing responsibilities in your job(s).

If you have gaps in your work history, are changing careers, or are not in what some employers view as a "favorable age group," you probably should use the *functional* or *hybrid* format. These styles focus more on skills than on any specific order or dates.

Functional Format

A **functional resume** (see Exhibit 2.2) lists your information under skill headings without necessarily focusing on dates. The main section of a functional resume is titled "Qualifications Summary," "Skills Composite," or something similar. Beneath this heading, you list your specific skills under subtitles such as "Administration," "Technical," "Sales," "Supervisory," "Marketing," and "Computer." Beneath the subtitles are brief descriptions that demonstrate your abilities in those areas. Specific examples and results that you produced are especially important (this is true for all styles of resumes). For example, "Increased sales production by 40 percent," "Reduced employee turnover by 15 percent," "Designed promotional program that resulted in an increase in our customer base from 265 to 345." Begin each statement with an action verb that emphasizes the skill you want to sell. Refer to the list of action verbs on page 62 when you write your skills summary.

Hybrid Format

The **hybrid style** is a combination of the chronological and functional formats (see Exhibit 2.3). As in the functional resume, you list functional, transferable skills that you can offer an employer, but unlike in the chronological style, you can give time periods (number of years rather than dates) for the jobs you've held. When a purely functional resume is used, except in applications for middle- and upper-management positions, employers sometimes tend to be a little suspicious and assume the applicant may be hiding a lack of skills or experience. Including the number of years of experience helps to keep them from prejudging you for not having shown a chronological job history. I asked my friend Jane Turk, who has been a human resources manager for many years (including seven years as a major recruiter for Martin Marietta in Denver, Colorado), if she would consider only those resumes with dates and reject the ones without. She said, "Of course not. If I see that the applicant has valid skills and experience for the position for which he or she is applying, I will call them for an interview." Giving dates is *essential*, however, when the skills you are selling relate to a field that changes rapidly, such as Internet programming. In this situation employers need to know that your skills and experience are up to date.

If you choose the hybrid format, you can include dates of employment under the Employment History heading if you are not fearful of revealing job gaps or your age. Whether to reveal your age can be an important decision. Some

EXHIBIT 2.1   Chronological resume.

ANN CONNELL

4021 West 120th Avenue
Westminster, Colorado 80235

(303) 541-7866
ACONNELL@AOL.COM

Professional Objective
Long-term employment that allows for advancement in both learning potential and professional development within the drafting field. Am open to residential and/or commercial design.

Qualifications

CAD Operation—Completed training on "virtual reality" software, invested 300 hours in lab study. Am knowledgeable in AutoCAD 14 and 2000.

Architectural Drafting and Design—Created models and architectural drawings for urban design, also researched applications for federal grants, and made final sketches accompanied by notes and specified dimensions.

Specifications Writing—Rendered directions and explanations of architectural plans for use by contractors and other on-site building personnel, prepared program development reports regarding cost analysis and building code analysis, and assisted with design proposals for low-cost housing for senior citizens.

Employment History

Gerold Mills Architectural Associates, Littleton, Colorado, 2007–Present
Architect
Was responsible for urban design of large-scale architectural projects and site plans that shaped an urban environment. Created and rendered urban design plans and concepts.

Norwalk Architects, Denver, Colorado, 2005–2007
Began as draftsperson and was promoted to Senior Draftsperson.
CAD and board design plus writing specifications for use by contractors for low-cost housing.

Education

University of Colorado, Boulder, Colorado, Graduate, Architecture degree, 2007.
Internship with Howdershell Planners, Westminster, Colorado.

Bay Valley Technical Institute, Hays, Kansas, Associate's degree in Architectural Drafting, 2005.

Licensed: State of Colorado
Membership: American Association of Architects

MATTHEW ALLEN

2102 West 153rd Avenue, New York, NY 10024
(212) 567-3000, Cell: (212) 340-9080
mallen@evernet.com

OBJECTIVE

A position in the field of Electronics, prefer Satellite/Communications Systems related.
FIVE-YEAR CAREER GOAL: Communications Analysis Management.

SUMMARY OF QUALIFICATIONS

Electronics Applications—*Four years.* Installed, maintained, transferred, and repaired
2-way radios, telecommunications, electronic, and data equipment. Experience with electrical controls, circuit construction and applications.

Computer Applications—*Three years.* Computer programming and microprocessors to
include UNIX and C++ programming.

Mathematics—*Four years.* Performed daily algebraic/geometric and trigonometric calculations with emphasis in Electronic Communications systems.

Teamwork—*Seven years.* Worked on diverse teams in different applications stemming
from military career, electronic employment, and the mechanical aspect of maintenance
repair in the communications industry.

EDUCATION

New York Institute of Electronics, New York, NY, 2008
Associate's degree with double major: Computer Programming and Electronics Emphasis in
programming, microprocessors, electronic applications with enhanced troubleshooting skills.
GPA: 3.9 with Honors. Peer Counselor Team member, Tutor for Algebra, Trigonometry,
and Computer Programming/Assembly. Perfect Attendance.

University of California, Irvine, Irvine, California, 2005
Completed Veterans' Upward-Bound Program with advanced studies in Mathematics,
Science, and English. 120 clock hours.

EMPLOYMENT BACKGROUND

Arrow Electronics, New York, New York

G.I.N. Rentals, Irvine, California

Astech, Division of Electronic Research, Irvine, California

United States Navy, San Diego, California

REFERENCES

Professional references are available upon request

EXHIBIT 2.3   Hybrid resume.

EDWARD F. MARTINEZ

9803 Aspen Road, Thornton, Colorado 80229

(303) 252-9187, Cell: (303) 367-9023, efmartinez@rockynet.net

OBJECTIVE:	A position in the medical field, preferably as a Medical Assistant in a free-standing emergency center or a fast-paced medical office.
SKILLS SUMMARY:	Training in the processing of insurance claim forms, surgical procedures, EKG and radiology, front and back office procedures, computer applications including DOS, Excel, WordPerfect, Windows, and Medisoft. Typing speed of 55 wpm.
EDUCATION:	Parks Junior College, Thornton, Colorado 2008 Associate's degree in Medical Assisting, GPA: 3.9 (4.0) Internship: University of Colorado Medical Center University of Northern Colorado, Greeley, Colorado 2006 Completed 100 credit hours in Biology/Human Anatomy and Pre-chiropractic Medicine.
EMPLOYMENT:	COMPUTER ROOM ASSISTANT, Parks Junior College 4/07 to present. Data entry, running programs and printing rosters. JOB COACH, Shafer Rehabilitation Center, Denver, Colorado 12/04 – 4/07. Helped in the instruction of mentally disabled adults in learning how to work in the community. VETERINARY ASSISTANT, New Life Center, Fort Collins, Colorado. 1/02–12/04. Front office duties of answering phones, making appointments, billing and filing. Back office responsibilities of assisting in surgery, removing sutures, giving injections, and sterilizing equipment.
ACHIEVEMENTS:	Alpha Beta Kappa Director's List for GPA of 3.5 or above Perfect Attendance Awards Colorado State Scholarship recipient
REFERENCES:	See attached reference letters.

employers may subscribe to myths such as "If you're under the age of 25, you're unstable" or "If you're over 55, you are over the hill." Kenneth Terrell in his article in the *U.S. News & World Report,* "When Experience Counts, Older Workers Are Finding a Welcome in the Job Market," states that many people ages 50 and older—"experienced workers" in human resources jargon—are planning to work past traditional retirement ages."[1]

The American Association of Retired Persons (AARP) November/ December 2007 issue of the magazine published an article honoring employers who have created workplaces for their 50+ employees. They included a list of the "Best Employers for Workers Over 50." Anyone interested in finding companies honored by AARP for valuing older workers (50+) can go to www.aarpmagazine.org/money.[2]

No one in *any age group* need be concerned if they present themselves positively and enthusiastically. Even though discrimination against applicants based on age is illegal, you would be amazed at how many employers disregard this law. Job gaps, as long as they are not extreme and you have justifiable reasons for them, are not as serious as most people think. In my experience, I have found very few people who haven't had some gaps in their work background for various reasons.

Targeted Format

A focused presentation of accomplishments and skill areas directed toward a specific job or career is known as a **targeted resume** (see Exhibit 2.4). This kind of resume may be in the chronological, the functional, or the hybrid format, but the difference is that it includes the actual title of the job or career you are seeking instead of a job objective (discussed in the next section).

The targeted resume looks like any of the other formats, except that it is *more focused* and includes information directly related to the targeted job. This format is especially effective when you are interested in a specific job and when you need separate resumes for different career paths.

Video Resume

In my research and speaking with employers, I discovered a different kind of resume now being used by people seeking jobs called the video resume. According to Joe Turner, a 16-year recruiter who finds and places people in jobs, it is a good tool and he found that employers would definitely look at a video resume.[3]

To create your video resume, you only need a video recorder or a digital camera. *Caution: Be certain you use common sense and make it professional.* It is not the place to try out your comedy routines. In some of the videos I have viewed, some job seekers have been posting their videos directly to YouTube and MySpace. My online guru Jane keeps me updated with items that are posted on YouTube and MySpace. Whatever you think about those websites, they are viewed by a lot of people, so it is another method of getting more exposure.

Electronic Format

Whatever style of resume you decide to use—chronological, functional, hybrid, video, or targeted—an electronic resume is different only in the way it is laid out on the page and in the wording. It is formatted so that you can send it via e-mail

EXHIBIT 2.4   Targeted resume.

DAVID A. WILLIAMS

19271 East Ellen Avenue, Aurora, Colorado 80012   •   (303) 366-6933   •   dawilliams@msn.com

JOB TARGET: PERSONNEL & LABOR RELATIONS SPECIALIST

EDUCATION

UNIVERSITY OF TUCSON, Tucson, Arizona 2007
Bachelor of Arts: Business Administration, Minor in Industrial & Labor Relations, GPA: 3.7/4.0

Phoenix School of Business, Phoenix, Arizona
Completed 24 semester hours in Economics and Labor Relations.

RELATED CAPABILITIES

- Written and Oral Communication Skills
- Research & Development of Labor Policies
- Independent Decision-Making Ability
- Patience and Diplomacy
- Good Judgment

EXPERIENCE

RESEARCH ASSISTANT, 9/2007 to Present
A & M Research Services, Aurora, Colorado
Currently doing market research on the union and labor relations in the supermarket industry.
Design client surveys, interpret research data, and prepare final reports.

PLACEMENT ASSISTANT, 2004 to 9/2007
University of Tucson, Tucson, Arizona
Prepared job lead reports, corresponded with students and client companies. Proficient in
Microsoft Word. Procured job leads for students from telephone cold calling. *Contributed to an
increase in student job placement by 20%.*

PERSONNEL ASSISTANT, 1999 to 2004
U.S. Army, Phoenix, Arizona
Assisted with interviews and paperwork of inductees for job placement. *Acted as a grievance
mediator for enlistees.*

PROFESSIONAL AFFILIATIONS

Member of American Society for Personnel Administration, Aurora, Colorado Chapter,
1998 to present. Chapter Research Coordinator.

GOALS: MBA and Graduate Field Work in Labor Relations.

INTERESTS: The history of unions and the progression of labor contract negotiations.

REFERENCES: Please see attached letters of reference:
- A & M Research Services, R & D Director, George M. Silky.
- University of Tucson, Student Services & Affairs Administration, Dr. Lloyd Burns.
- Additional references will be provided upon request.

or post it on the Internet. Instead of emphasizing your skills and accomplishments with action verbs, you must use nouns as keywords that will be recognized by the employers' software that scans it for matches to the advertised opening. In most cases, employers prefer resumes to be submitted in plain text (also called ASCII text or MS-DOS text). However, this is not to say your resume will always be received if written in that format. Specific instructions for formatting, printing, and sending all styles of resumes are given later in this chapter (see "The Final Draft").

Points to Remember for All Resumes

Give facts, figures, results, quantitative descriptions

Employers are not impressed with obscure and vague phrases such as "I am a great problem solver, a hard worker, and detail oriented." Almost all applicants *say* these things but give no proof to support them. Employers see these empty words on hundreds of resumes, and they are meaningless unless you back them up with specific examples. Tell the prospective employer where and when you obtained skills and how long you performed them. When you claim to have an attitude or attribute, such as being "detail oriented" or "a hard worker," give a specific example of a time you demonstrated or were praised for that attribute.

Your resume should be original and have a personality—yours

Don't be afraid of deviating from the norm or of being innovative enough to go beyond the typical ways that people design their resumes. A word of caution, however: Keep in mind that employers in industries other than the arts, communication, or sales are usually a bit conservative and might not be receptive to a very unusual resume, such as one done in hand lettering or one that looks like a page out of a magazine advertisement. In the field of art or design, this kind of resume may be regarded as creative and be well received, whereas employers in other fields may see it as unprofessional. One document, the Portfolio, which you can add to your job searching package (discussed in Chapter 3) gives you the opportunity to be innovative. When you are writing your resume, however, always use good judgment and taste and never lose sight of the professional aspect in presenting your qualifications to the prospective employer. Stay away from cutesy gimmicks and don't get carried away with the unusual or bizarre. Get several persons' opinions, particularly from those already in your field. If your college has a career assistance department, ask for suggestions and advice from those personnel because they are in touch with the employers who hire, and they know what employers prefer to see on resumes. In addition, if you are writing an electronic resume, be certain to follow the guidelines for that format, including the individual employer's requirements.

Writing the First Draft

s soon as you have compiled all of your background information and have chosen the resume style best suited to your job objective, you are ready to begin writing the first draft. Unless it is obvious that your employment history and education are directly related to the position(s) you'll be applying for, include a job objective. You do not want to make your reader guess at what you want to do.

Job Objective

The **job objective** is a brief statement telling the employer what type of position you are seeking, and it always appears at the beginning of the resume, immediately after your name and address. It can also contain a short sentence mentioning your long-term employment goals. Objectives seem to be somewhat difficult for most people to write because they just don't know where to begin. Often, they either don't say anything meaningful at all or get so wordy that the reader is turned off before even getting into the resume. Other job objectives are so general that they have a cookie-cutter look, and the employer suspects that they have been copied from a sample resume. If it appears that the applicant either didn't take the time to construct a coherent job objective or doesn't know what it is he or she wants to do, the employer may conclude that the applicant lacks initiative.

As you write your objective, keep one idea firmly in mind: "What do I want to do; what is my job goal?" This will help to keep you on track and focused so you avoid rambling. I suggest that you not use words like "challenging" or "rewarding" because they are so overused and abstract that they mean little to the reader. Be very careful of using phrases such as "advancement into management." Management of what? Sales? Production? Administration? Personnel? Computer operations? Vague words only reveal to the employer that you haven't done your research to learn what the career path is for your field or you *really don't know where you want to be in the future.* Although your objective should be concise, you do want to keep it a little general so as not to disqualify yourself from being considered for related positions that the employer may have open. This is especially important if you are just entering your field and do not have an abundance of experience for the position for which you are applying. Try to avoid using specific job titles unless you are targeting one. In this event, you would probably be better off using a targeted format and wouldn't need an objective.

Your choice of words is important because of the pictures they paint for your reader and the assumptions he or she will draw from them. Be certain that the words you use are clear to the reader. To avoid being misunderstood, avoid using abstract words (ones that can be interpreted in different ways). Here are a few examples of different ways to write job objectives. Some of the sample resumes in this chapter also include job objectives.

Banquet Manager with responsibilities in food preparation, purchasing, staff development, and menu planning.

Long-term goal: General Manager of Hotel Operations

Editorial position, preferably within the textbook department of a publishing company.

Communications specialist preparing news releases, designing and editing brochures, displays, and posters, and executing advertising strategies.

Long-term goal: Director of Public Relations

Researcher/technical writer for a communications company devoted to the advancement of information technology.

A position in physical therapy that involves treatment planning, use of therapeutic modalities, and follow-up care for patients.

To associate with a company in information systems management with software development and specialized utility programs.

Seeking full- or part-time employment as instructor in networking administration, electronics, or programming.

Once you've written your job objective, the next step is to decide what information to present first. Many resumes begin with a section titled "Summary of Qualifications" (or some similar appropriate title) that summarizes your skills, up front, for the reader. This saves the reader from having to search through the resume to discover what you have to offer. If you need more information to help you write this part, review the functional format description given earlier.

The order in which you present your qualifications is critical because you have only about 30 seconds or less to convince your readers that you have what they are looking for. When you consider the large number of resumes that employers and human resources people have to read, it's not surprising they will be scanning by the time they are halfway down the page. So if you want to be considered for an interview, you had better give them your best shot right up front.

After the summary of qualifications, most resumes give either a section on employment experience or one listing education. If your education is what most qualifies you for the position, present it first. However, if your experience is your best selling point, begin there.

Education Section

Under the heading of "Education," include all relevant training you have had, whether it was from a formal institution, on the job, or elsewhere. Now, you're probably thinking, "How the heck do I know what is relevant?" Obviously, anything directly related to the position you are applying for is relevant. In addition, take a look at the functional aspects of the position: It quite possibly requires skills such as the ability to communicate, to handle conflict and stress, to take initiative and action, to think strategically, and, almost always, to be flexible. These qualifications may not be stated specifically in the ad or job description, but in today's workplace, they are almost always necessary to the performance of any job. Consequently, if you have training or experience in these kinds of functional skills, they would certainly be relevant.

Begin by listing the name(s) of the institution(s) you attended after high school; high school data are included only if the data are not outdated and there were awards, courses, or relevant (there's that word again) accomplishments that would reinforce your credibility to perform the job. Naming *all* of the classes you have taken is a needless waste of time and space and very boring to read, so don't do it. Your transcript will provide these details, and employers will request one if they feel it is important. It is necessary only to list areas of concentration or majors with emphasis on certain subjects. Include the city and state where the institution is located; do not give street addresses, phone numbers, and ZIP codes.

If you attended college and did not graduate, but completed some courses that are—you guessed it—relevant, then include information about the college. By all means, if you do list it, be sure to include what you studied there. An effective way to state this is to give the college name and add "Completed (number) of semester/quarter/clock hours in (course or subject name)." By writing it this way, you don't indicate that you quit but that you *completed* a certain number of hours in that subject.

A frequently asked question is whether to include your grade point average (GPA) on your resume. This is definitely optional; however, some employers have told me they like to see it. If you leave it off, an employer might wonder how bad your grades really were, but if it is 3.0 or above, by all means do so. However, if you decide to include it and it is below 3.0, be sure to explain in your cover letter any extenuating circumstances that prevented you from earning a higher average. Maybe you worked a full-time job while you were in school, or you are a single parent with children to care for; any *valid* situation that may have diverted your efforts to maintain a higher GPA would be credible. This can sometimes be advantageous for you as it shows you are capable of applying yourself and finishing what you set out to do, regardless of the disadvantages. Another option is to list your major GPA or your average grades for only the classes taken in your major.

In a functional resume, dates of attendance and graduation are usually not given. In all the other styles, dates of attendance are not important, but the date of graduation from school is important if your curriculum was technical because it indicates that your skills are current. The key is to be consistent in all areas and styles.

Employment History Section

In this part of the resume, there are different rules for the chronological and the functional styles. If the chronological style is the best choice for your background, list your present or most recent job and continue backward for all jobs that you have decided to include. The big question is, "How far back should I go?" For managerial jobs, limit your experience to 15 years. About 10 years is usually sufficient for tech positions unless positions you held earlier would give additional proof of your ability to do the job. In this case, rather than filling pages with your employment history, you should probably choose a functional or hybrid resume style. If you are using the chronological style and want to inform the employer of the skills you acquired in those earlier positions, you can do so by adding a few lines about them in your cover letter or add them under a heading of "Other Experience." Briefly explain and do not include dates. (How to do this is explained in the section "Cover Letters.")

When you are listing your jobs in the chronological format, do not repeat the same job descriptions over and over if you have held several similar positions for different companies. This parroting of material is one of the major objections to chronological resumes; it makes them repetitive and often boring to read. Simply name the position(s) you held, briefly describe the duties and responsibilities, then list the companies and dates of employment. If you are using the hybrid format, list the companies, and if you choose, the dates or number of years you were there. (See Exhibit A.5 in the appendix.) Whenever you list a company, if its line of business is not obvious from the name, include a brief description.

When you list dates on your resume, don't worry about weeks and days; round all time spans up or down to a number of months and years. If you were at a job less than six months, think about whether it should even be on the resume. Is it relevant to the position you are now seeking? What do you do if you have held a lot of part-time or contract jobs that were for short periods of time, and they show skills that prove you can perform the job you seek? In this case, list the jobs under a subtitle such as "Part-Time Jobs."

If you are a new graduate and need to intensify your experience, show every work experience you've had including internships (paid and unpaid), student jobs, coop education, and even extracurricular activities. If you've been out of the workforce for a few years as a home manager or on a sabbatical, list transferable skills you gained in volunteer, civic, hobby, and household work.

Things that you *do not* put on your resume in the Employment section are reasons for leaving past jobs, past salaries, and present salary requirements. These items can be discussed in the interview or in the cover letter if the employer has requested them.

Related Professional Experience

Include a section with this title if you have relevant experience that you gained by doing volunteer work or some specialized skill(s) that would be of benefit to the prospective employer. If the experience or training is far removed from your job objective or the requirements of the job for which you are applying, leave it out. For example, if you took a course in underwater basket weaving or belly dancing, leave that out unless it is relevant to the position.

Additional Headings

Anything you haven't already included but that illustrates your special qualities and enhances your marketability can be stated in a separate section with its own title. Here are some possible titles:

Professional Licenses, Certifications

Publications

Professional Organization Memberships

Foreign Languages (be sure to indicate degree of fluency)

Awards, Travel

Personal Information

Except in rare occasions, personal information is not required on resumes. Since the inception of the EEOC (Equal Employment Opportunity Commission), it is illegal for any employer to select an employee based on this kind of information. *Only if employers can prove a job requires specific personal qualifications, can they require that you submit this information.* For example, you must be 21 years of age to sell alcohol. Even if personal information is requested, you do not need to put it on your resume. You will provide it later when you have been offered the job. Pictures are used only if requested for certain occupations. Do not list your age, sex, marital status, religion, place of birth, state of health, social security number, or any other personal information on your resume. Including it simply gives an employer the opportunity to prejudge you or to discriminate against you. Also, if you are posting it online, you don't want to give identity thieves the opportunity to steal yours. If an employer does request personal information before a job offer, the request may be illegal. Illegal inquiries of this nature are very sensitive subjects. How to handle this kind of questioning professionally is explained in Chapter 4 in the discussions of application forms and interviewing.

References

A few years ago, we advised that the section on a resume listing references was fading into extinction like the dinosaurs because of the controversy concerning a person's right to privacy and because many times, background checks were unreliable. Employers hesitated to give out any information except job titles and time worked because they feared being sued for defamation of character. Most of the time, when an employer is reading your resume, he or she is not interested in your references. Only after the employer has interviewed you and has an interest in hiring you will he or she take the time to call or write for references. What we have now, however, is an increase in reference checking with former employers because prospective new employers are afraid of setting themselves up for litigation should they hire someone who turns out to have a history of theft, child or spousal abuse, violence, or any other negatives in their past. I would still maintain that the request for references almost always occurs at the time of interviewing when the employer has decided you would be a viable employee.

To avoid the risk of lawsuits by former employees who receive poor references, many companies now instruct their employees not to give out any references at all. In most states, recent court cases have expanded employees' rights to sue employers, so employers are still very concerned about charges of slander or libel.

Some companies only verify dates of employment. I'm told by a long-time employee of Qwest that they refer all reference requests to the human resources department, which only verifies dates of employment, position held, and wages. Another method employers are using is to have the person leaving the company sign a release that gives the employer the right to speak truthfully. For some positions, however, employers do check motor vehicle or credit records. Liz Pulliam Weston, who has a website, "Your Money Message Board," says that "Many employers—including the federal government—routinely scour credit reports on current and prospective employees to help decide who's hired or fired."[4] Increasingly employers are using professional background checkers such as Avert, Inc., which is based in Fort Collins, Colorado. Avert is a nationwide company with 600 couriers who tap databases in all 3,300 counties in the United States for public information about applicants. This company provides employment screening products (some automated) to facilitate verification of references, social security numbers, criminal records, and credit reports. Employers have learned that this information, however, is only as accurate as the data input because it may not reveal records in counties, cities, or states where the applicant has lived and worked. It may not give a complete account of a prospective applicant.

Despite the success of some employees' lawsuits, be aware that you can't sue an employer unless you have proof that the reference information or comment was knowingly false, disclosed for a malicious purpose, or violated your civil rights. To avoid unpleasant surprises, you can check your own references before your job search through a company like DRC (Documented Reference Check, Inc., www.badreferences.com), based in Diamond Bar, California. DRC has checked backgrounds for thousands of job seekers nationwide. Or if it is your credit history you are concerned about, you may want to write to one of the following credit bureaus to get a copy of your credit record. You are entitled to a free copy of your file.

- Equifax, 1-800-685-1111
- EXPERIAN (formerly TRW) offers a credit check monitoring service where membership gives you alerts of changes in your credit history and supplies forms and tips for disputes, 1-888-397-3742.
- Trans-Union, National Consumer Disclosure Center, 1-800-916-8800
- If you go to the Experian website, you will find an offer for all three reports from the top three credit reporting agencies. It is labeled "FREE 3 BUREAU CREDIT REPORT" and it asks for your personal information, name, address, phone number, and so on. Then it asks for a credit card number and a $1.00 fee.

If you happen to have a credit history that needs repair, you can write for a free booklet called *Getting Back in the Black* from FTC Public Reference Branch, Room 130, Sixth Street & Pennsylvania Avenue NW, Washington, DC 20580. The FTC's Web address is www.ftc.gov. According to the Fair Credit Reporting Act (FCRA), you should also know that employers need your permission to run a credit check, so failing to do so is an FCRA violation, and they are supposed to tell you if credit information is used against you. *Reality check:* Not all employers are totally honest when it comes to leveling with you.

If you absolutely feel the need to include a Reference section on your resume, a short statement such as "References will be provided upon request" is sufficient. However, because everyone knows that you will provide references if asked, this statement is rather pointless (especially if putting it in your resume means adding a second page).

Whether you include a References section on your resume or not, always be prepared to supply the names, addresses, e-mail addresses, and phone numbers of at least three or four credible references. Have a reference page, typed and ready, that lists people who can vouch for your character. (See the sample reference list in Exhibit 2.5.) Use the names of professional friends and acquaintances; for example, teachers, clergy, or former employers and coworkers who have known you for at least one to three years. Friends and family members usually do not qualify as references. **Be sure to notify and ask permission from the people you are listing as references. Send them a copy of your resume so they can have it in front of them when they are providing a reference.**

Although a list of references probably does not belong in your resume, *reference letters* are a different matter. If you have current ones from college professors or former employers, for example, and they are excellent testimony to your skill level and good character, you may wish to attach copies of them to your resume. Letters of commendation about notable volunteer services that you have performed are also worth including. Attach no more than two or three letters. If possible, reproduce them on the same kind of paper you use for your resume and cover letter. (See the sample reference letters in Exhibits 2.6 and 2.7.)

With good reference letters and a list of references you can hand the employer, you can save yourself and the employer a lot of time and trouble. Alternatively, you may wish to call or write your reference people and ask them to send reference letters directly to the employer.

REFERENCE PAGE

List your references here—at least three or four professional acquaintances. Have this list available for filling out application forms and for the interview, should the employer request it.

Name and Title	Company Name/Address	Telephone/E-Mail

JANE BRYANT

REFERENCES

Ms. Mary Kay Brown
Human Resource Director
Canco Manufacturing Company
123 Jewell Street
San Diego, California 92010
(714) 461-8111
kaybrown@canco.com

Mr. Joseph Blue
Owner
Pacific Insurance, Inc.
8917 "G" Street
San Diego, California 92102
(714) 442-0331
joeblue@pacific.com

Mrs. Betty Paige
Instructor
Needmore Union Adult School
1211 Morrison Street
San Diego, California 92022
(714) 579-2810
betty_paige@needmore_union.com

Cynthia Blaine
Supervisor
Avery Structures, Inc.
6945 E. 112th Avenue
Suite 349
Seattle, Washington 98109
(206) 424-8987
cblaine@avery.com

KANE ENGINEERING

40526 N. Industrial Lane, Pasadena, California 90406   (818) 555-1234   www.kane.com

Mr. Gregory Mason
Coronet Co.
8711 W. 14th Street
Pasadena, CA 90401

April 14, 2008

Dear Mr. Mason:

John Reddick has been employed with my company for two years. He is extremely efficient and quick to learn the procedures to keep up with the fast pace we required of him. His ability to comprehend what was needed before my direction allowed me to focus on my own responsibilities. He is customer focused and learned the company's short-term and long-term goals.

John's time working for Kane Engineering was enjoyable and will be an experience of which I will have positive memories.

Sincerely,

John Kane

John Kane
President

KANE ENGINEERING

40526 N. Industrial Lane, Pasadena, California 90406   (818) 555-1234   www.kane.com

April 14, 2008

To Whom It May Concern:

John Reddick's work with me has been far above average. He has been on time and available, allowing me to keep up with the demands of my customers. He has been adaptable and willing to meet any training requirements that we together have recognized as necessary. He has shared new technical advancements in computer networking that he learned through his degree program at Westwood College of Technology. He has many times agreed to work overtime or come in on his days off to cover for other employees.

Sincerely,

John Kane

John Kane
President

P.S. Please feel free to call me at (818) 555-1234 or contact me via e-mail at john_kane@kane.com for any additional information you would like.

The Final Draft

N ow for the fun stuff! When you've done all the detail work of compiling your information, chosen your format, written your first draft (and maybe the second or third?), it is time to write your final draft. Next you organize and rewrite all of this material so that you will have a resume you will be proud to distribute to prospective employers. It's at this point that some people even get an ego stroke when they realize what talented and skilled people they really are. Often, when I prepare resumes for clients and they look at the final draft, they exclaim, "Wow, I didn't realize I had so much to offer!"

As you read the following guidelines, look at the sample resumes on pages 35–39 and the additional examples in the appendix. (These resumes are for fictitious applicants, and the information is imaginary. Any resemblance to actual persons is coincidental.)

Completing the Final Draft

The following instructions are appropriate for the majority of hard copy resumes. The rules are different for electronic resumes, which are designed to be scanned by computer into a database. Specific instructions for the electronic format appear later in this chapter.

Stay with basic color choices for paper

Use standard 8.5 by 11-inch white, ivory, light gray, or light blue paper. For those fields in which color and style are key factors, such as the art and design fields, this rule may not apply. In addition, printers and office supply places offer special paper with backgrounds that are quite unique and pleasant to the eye. Just remember to avoid anything that is extreme. Too many job seekers labor under the false illusion that printing a resume on brightly colored paper will draw attention to it. This may be true, but you want employers to be drawn to your resume because you match what they're looking for, not because the color of the paper hurts their eyes. During my years in career development, I have seen just about every color you can imagine; it didn't help anyone to get an interview.

Use an appealing format and layout

Type should be spaced so that the resume has an all-around balanced appearance. Double- or triple-space between sections and use spacing sparingly within sections. Margins should be from 1 to 1.5 inches. If you do not have a lot of information and you would have difficulty filling a page, *evenly* increase the size of the margins and the spacing between sections. If you have a little more than would go on one page and rewording or deleting would create confusion for your reader, you can decrease the margins to 0.5 inch. However, when keeping your resume to one page requires that you reduce the white space so much that the page looks messy and crowded, it is better to use wider margins and go to two pages rather than to cram it onto one page. Aim for a "picture frame" look and an easy-to-read design.

Keep it concise

Preferably, resumes should be no longer than two pages, except in special cases where it is necessary to provide additional information required by an employer (e.g., government and education). Many employers say they prefer one-page resumes, but, again, do not condense your resume to one page at the expense of readability.

Make your resume inviting and easy to read

Highlight important points that you especially want noticed by CAPITALIZ-ING, **bolding,** or <u>underscoring</u>. Don't force your readers to "dig" for the information; they won't.

Control the quality

Your resume should be typed and saved on a computer and printed out using a printer with letter-quality output. The print should be dark enough and large enough so that it can be read easily. Once you have a master copy that is bright and clear, take it to a printer for reproduction. Or, if you own a quality printer, print out as many copies as you need. Just be certain that the copies you distribute are bright and clear.

Identify subsequent pages

If your resume is on two pages, place a heading on the second page that includes your name and "Page 2" about 1 to 2 inches from the top. (Most word processing software programs begin your page at the proper number of lines from the top of the page, so begin where you see the cursor.) Either of the following styles is acceptable:

Larue R. Austin   2   (date, optional)

Larue R. Austin

Page 2

After this heading, drop down two to four lines to continue your resume information.

Always be accurate and never fudge or lie

U.S. News & World Report has reported that "a surprising number of applicants are telling whoppers on their resumes." According to the article, Jude M. Werra, a Wisconsin headhunter, "checks the education claims on the 300 or so executive resumes he gets annually. In the first six months of this year, 23 percent of his applicants awarded themselves fictitious degrees, up from 17 percent last year." The article reports that this is happening with applicants from janitors to nurses. Werra says he is puzzled because "you don't need to lie. It's also risky because checking is easier than ever."[5] You are going to have to substantiate your information in the interview and on the application form, so be careful of your claims. If there are negatives in your past such as some serious job hopping or you left a job on bad terms, it's okay to leave dates off and stick to the positives that were there in the job. Just remember what I said previously: You are going to have to back up what you put on the resume if you get called in for an interview.

Forgo the title

A title (such as "Resume" or "Resume of Qualifications") is unnecessary. Your reader is quite aware of what the document is. A little humor here: You don't put "Letter" at the top of your letters, do you?

Keep it flat

When you mail or drop off your resume to a prospective employer, place it in a 9 by 12- or 10 by 13-inch envelope. If you fold it to fit a smaller envelope, you risk having creases that could blur the print. A resume looks more professional if it has not been folded.

Be extremely cautious of using negatives

Anything that could be interpreted as criticism, conflict, or hostility should not be on your resume, or anywhere else in the job search, for that matter. Be careful about including information that could cause employers to stereotype you. For example, listing an interest in and expertise with weapons of any kind may project an image that an employer could find unfavorable if you are applying for a job unrelated to gun or weapon use. With the incidences of so many murders on college campuses and the controversy about illegal gun ownership, this kind of information placed on a resume could eliminate you from a lot of job interviews.

Proofread

Last but not least, before you make any copies, have at least three people proofread your resume, preferably a school counselor or someone in your industry. At least one of these people should have good grammatical skills. If you want to be called for an interview, your resume has to be error free, smudge free, visually appealing, and professional.

Completing the Electronic Resume

The final draft of your electronic resume[6] (see Exhibit 2.8) should follow most of the guidelines for conventional resumes. Because it must be scanned and sent via e-mail, however, some special instructions apply. These involve the use of keywords that will be recognized by the employer's database, and preparation in a format that can be electronically transmitted and scanned.

A resume to be posted to an employer's online resume template or scanned into a database must be prepared and saved as a text-only document. Text-only documents can contain very little formatting, so they are visually not as appealing as paper resumes. Fonts, bolding, italics, brackets, borders, tables, headers, footers, inconsistent tab layout, and underlining are all off-limits because they can make the document difficult for the software to read. Saving your resume in rich-text format (RTF) will preserve all the formatting, but some employers' software may not be able to read it. So if you want to get the most responses to your electronic resume, save it as a text-only file.

The organization of an electronic resume is also somewhat different from that of the paper resume. The margin and white-space guidelines are the same, but don't use centered headings, only flush-left text. Because you can't use bolding or different fonts, type your headings in all capital letters to make them stand out. The best fonts to use are Helvetica, Times, Courier, and Arial, and the point size should be no smaller than 12.

NAME: JEAN KRAMER

JOB TITLE: INSTRUCTOR OF ENGLISH AND CAREER DEVELOPMENT

SKILLS SUMMARY

[Summarize your strongest skills and strengths using keywords—nouns, not verbs.]

Classroom and workshop instruction, communication: oral and written, job search skills, counseling, student and client job placement, newsletter production and design, special events coordination, tutor: vocabulary and English as a second language (ESL), owner/manager of career counseling and job placement business, Microsoft Word, Excel, Powerpoint, WordPerfect, Pagemaker.

JEAN KRAMER

jkramer@gpcom.net

(303) 555-6968

Note: *Street address omitted due to privacy concerns*

JOB OBJECTIVE *[State your immediate job goal and long-term goals if you wish.]*

Instructor of Career Development and/or English Grammar and Composition

EXPERIENCE   *[List jobs held that support the position desired, beginning with present or most recent and working in reverse order.]*

Westwood College of Technology, Denver, Colorado. 2004–Present
Instructor/Job Search Skills Counselor
English Grammar and Composition, Job Search Skills, Human Relations, Psychology, Technical Writing.

Control Data Institute, Denver, Colorado. 2000–2004
Student Services Administrator
Career Development instruction, part-time and full-time employment for students, coordination with financial aid and admissions departments to ensure student success and graduate placement, public relations events for the college.

Denver Institute of Technology, Denver, Colorado. 1995–2000
College Student Placement Director and Instructor
Career Development and Job Search Skills design and instruction, small business management and marketing instruction, full- and part-time employment for students, instructor hiring and training.

EXHIBIT 2.8   Continued

EDUCATION   *[List all relevant education, naming colleges, locations, and degrees and majors; include on-the-job training if it relates to your objective.]*

University of Colorado at Denver, Denver, Colorado
Master of Arts degree in English, minor in Secondary Education

University of California at Long Beach, Long Beach, California
Adjunct Professor Training in Vocabulary and English as a Second Language

Black Hills State College, Spearfish, South Dakota
Training in Methods and Techniques for Student Success

[OPTIONAL HEADINGS]

SPECIALIZED TRAINING *[those not covered in education section]*

Numerous workshops, seminars, and instructor training for career development, classroom instructor methods and techniques, business management, and student retention.

HONORS/AWARDS *[job-related are especially noteworthy]*

Employee of the Term, Westwood College of Technology, 2007

Teacher of the Year nomination, Association of Post-Secondary Schools and Colleges, 2004

Outstanding Student Advisor award, Denver Institute of Technology, 1999–2000

PUBLICATIONS *[if any; give name of publication, title, and date]*

REFERENCES
[Stating that your references will be provided is not necessary as employers will ask for them when and if they need them. Do not list your references on your resume.]

[page 2]

If you e-mail your resume, move your address and phone number to the bottom of the document. If they are at the top, the computer screen may be taken up with the e-mail header, your return address, date and time, and so on. If this is all the employer sees on the first page, he or she might not be inclined to read on. Mary B. Nemnich and Fred E. Jandt, authors of *Cyberspace Job Search Kit*, suggest that you

> put only your name and job title at the top of the resume as a heading rather than waste that first screen with a header and address. The top of your resume is the most critical as your reader should know who you are and what you do within a few seconds of reading your resume. Following the heading, you should write a summary. With only about 20 lines to work with on the first screen, it is imperative that you make a strong, favorable impression in those first few lines. . . . The summary paragraph should contain some of the main keywords that describe your skills. Thus, the first part of your resume will look something like this:

J. B. Seeker

Public Relations Specialist

Summary: Talented Public Relations Practitioner with more than 15 years of experience and a proven track record in community and media relations. Excellent writing skills. Facility with desktop publishing, including PageMaker, Quark, and Microsoft Publisher. Familiar with Microsoft Word and Windows. Motivational speaker. Adept at press relations and creative advertising. MA in Communication Studies, PR emphasis.[7]

An important element of an electronic resume is the use of **keywords,** specific words that an employer looks for when searching a resume database. Your electronic resume will be scanned to create an electronic representation that can be read into an automatic resume tracking system. The tracking system allows the employer to find resumes that include words indicating specific skills. Keywords are usually noun forms. To make sure your resume is selected by the tracking system, therefore, use nouns such as *electronics technician, computer programmer, physical therapy, network administration, leadership, flexibility,* and *teamwork.*

If you used verb forms in your paper resume, change them to noun forms for the electronic version. For example:

Verb forms	*Designed* micro-video components for surgical equipment, *charted* statistical data, *handled* all correspondence with suppliers, and *selected and purchased* parts and materials.
Noun forms	Senior draftsperson, micro-video design, parts and materials purchasing, statistical data charting, and supplier correspondence.

If you are not sure about the keywords that companies are using, go to the classified ads in your local newspapers. Nemnich and Jandt suggest that "a good place to find job descriptions with ideas for keywords is the O*NET, a listing of job titles, descriptions, and needed skills that's available in book form from JIST Publishing, Inc. at www.jist.com and online at www.doleta.gov/programs/onet/onet_hp.htm."[8]

The preceding instructions for writing the final draft of your electronic resume were adapted from several online sources, such as ResumeDoctor.com, and from Nemnich and Jandt's *Cyberspace Job Search Kit.* More excellent detailed advice for preparing an electronic resume can be found in Chapter 7 of Nemnich and Jandt's book.

RESUME CHECKLIST

☞ Is your name visibly placed at the top? If it's difficult to pronounce, have you given your reader a phonetic spelling?

☞ Have you included your *complete* address(es) and phone numbers (home, cell, pager, work)?

☞ Did you remember to include your e-mail address if you have one?

☞ If this is an electronic resume, are your address, phone numbers, etc., all on separate lines?

☞ Did you sell yourself by showing how you could be of benefit to the employer by listing previous accomplishments?

☞ Is your resume no more than two pages in length, or if it is longer, are you certain the page(s) are necessary?

☞ Is your text balanced on the page(s)?

☞ Is your resume concise, specific, and easy to read?

☞ Did you avoid using the first-person pronoun: "I," "me," "my"?

☞ Does it have information that is not relevant to your job objective? If so, remove it.

☞ Are your indentations, margins, and columns consistent?

☞ If this is a traditional resume, did you use action verbs to begin your sentences and phrases, and are your sentences brief, clear, and to the point?

☞ If this is an electronic resume, did you use nouns rather than verbs to describe your skills and accomplishments?

☞ Did you show progression, growth, and initiative in the positions you've held?

☞ Most important, have you had at least three people proof your resume for you?

Functional Skills Inventory

Whether you are writing your resume or selling yourself to an employer in an interview, knowing your functional skills can be an advantage. These are the skills that are required in all fields, positions, and companies. They can often fill in for other areas where you may be lacking. When surveyed, employers list, as a top priority, basic skills such as reading comprehension and writing ability. At the top of the list is the ability to get along well with others, especially in today's diversified workforce. Another common priority is that a potential employee be able to use sound judgment and possess problem-solving skills. I have heard from numerous employers over the years that they are usually willing to provide some training in technical areas, but they do not have the time to train someone in basic skill areas or to teach an employee how to get along with others. A few years ago, the CEO of Burger King was asked how important he thought it was to be able to get along well with others. The reply was, "One of the hardest things I have to do is to go to an employee who is an excellent worker and tell him or her that I have to fire him or her because he or she can't get along with the others in the company."

Being aware and knowledgeable about all your functional skills and using them to sell yourself could make the difference in your being chosen over another applicant who may have more experience or education. So, before you prepare your benefit statements or go to an interview, go through the following list, select the skills you have by placing a checkmark in the circle, and incorporate them into your paperwork. You will have some very useful tools to use when speaking with prospective employers.

ARTISTIC:

- ○ Expressiveness (the ability to use my body to express feelings)
- ○ Operate well in a free, unstructured, unsupervised environment
- ○ Have talent for drawing, drafting, or creative writing
- ○ Musical knowledge or apparel fashioning

ATHLETIC/OUTDOOR/TRAVEL:

- ○ Motor/physical coordination and agility
- ○ Skill in general sports, recreation
- ○ Skills in creating, planning, and organizing outdoor activities, such as traveling, cultivating growing things, or working with animals

DETAIL/FOLLOW-THROUGH:

- ○ Ability to follow detailed instructions
- ○ Expert at getting things done
- ○ Skilled at making arrangements for events and processes
- ○ Responsible (consistently tackle and complete tasks ahead of time)
- ○ Good at processing information, classifying, and clerical tasks

DEVELOPING/PLANNING/ORGANIZING/MANAGING:

- ○ Use a systematic approach to goal setting
- ○ Can establish effective priorities
- ○ Adept at policy making, designing projects, organizing others
- ○ Ability to bring people together in cooperative efforts
- ○ Can schedule, assign, and supervise others in their work

○ Experienced in monitoring others' output
○ Good in areas of maintenance and evaluating

INFLUENCING/PERSUADING:

○ Able to develop rapport/trust
○ Expertise in reasoning persuasively and developing thoughts
○ Ability to sell ideas or products
○ Recruiter of talent or leadership
○ Can arbitrate/mediate between contending parties

INSTRUCTING/INTERPRETING/GUIDING:

○ Able to teach and promote a learning environment and convey enthusiasm
○ Competent at giving advice
○ Encourage and help people to make their own discoveries
○ Can counsel and facilitate groups
○ Competent trainer

INTUITIVE/INNOVATIVE:

○ Highly imaginative, inventive, creative, perceptive, and innovative
○ Willing to experiment with new approaches
○ Can visualize relationships between apparently unrelated factors
○ Show sound judgment
○ Derive things from other ideas
○ Adaptable
○ Can visualize in three dimensions
○ Show foresight
○ Can recognize obsolescence

LANGUAGE/READING/WRITING/SPEAKING:

○ Am an avid reader
○ Can edit accurately and compose and communicate with clarity
○ Can explain concepts systematically
○ Possess verbal/written skills in foreign languages
○ Ability to describe people, places, concepts, or things
○ Skill in promotional and technical writing

LEADERSHIP:

- ⦾ Competent in taking managed risks
- ⦾ Can plan for and effect change
- ⦾ Unwilling to automatically accept status quo
- ⦾ Possess excellent decision-making skills
- ⦾ Can lead others with constructive criticism and feedback
- ⦾ Ability to guide and chair meetings and groups

NUMERICAL/FINANCIAL/ACCOUNTING:

- ⦾ Can perform rapid computations in my head or on a calculator
- ⦾ Can design budgets and manage accounts
- ⦾ Adept at cost analysis
- ⦾ Extremely economical
- ⦾ Bookkeeping/accounting skills
- ⦾ Can solve statistical problems correctly

OBSERVATION/LEARNING/PROBLEM SOLVING:

- ⦾ Highly observant of people, data, and things
- ⦾ Adept at troubleshooting
- ⦾ Can listen carefully
- ⦾ Am perceptive, learn quickly, and retain what I learn
- ⦾ Able to assess situations and problems accurately and provide effective solutions

PERFORMING:

- ⦾ Can demonstrate products, procedures, systems
- ⦾ Can perform before groups and stimulate enthusiasm, with a flair for showmanship
- ⦾ Play musical instruments
- ⦾ Can make people laugh
- ⦾ Acting ability
- ⦾ Adept at various sports
- ⦾ Able to conduct and direct affairs/ceremonies

RELATIONSHIPS:

- ⦾ Ability to meet people easily and interact freely with strangers
- ⦾ Treat people with consideration, politeness, and respect
- ⦾ Aware of others' needs and feelings

- ○ Able to listen to others' points of view with an open mind
- ○ Relate to all people regardless of sex, creed, or race

RESEARCH/INVESTIGATION/ANALYSIS:

- ○ Ability to survey, interview, and examine critically and effectively
- ○ Can perceive and define cause-and-effect relationships
- ○ Define problems; choose and evaluate options
- ○ Review and evaluate choices/options

TIPS ON WORDING

- Avoid the use of personal pronouns such as "I," "me," or "my." The subject of your sentences is obviously you, so it is redundant to use these pronouns repeatedly. Begin your sentences with action verbs, or in the electronic resume, use nouns to describe your qualifications.

- Use an outline format with short sentences; even sentence fragments are permissible if they are otherwise grammatically correct and they make sense.

- Focus on your accomplishments and what you can do for the employer, not on wordy, lengthy descriptions of job duties.

- Avoid abbreviations, especially if they might be misunderstood. Use only those that are universally known. Those used in addresses are permissible, but they look more professional when they are spelled out. My recommendation is that even the two-letter abbreviations for states should not be used on your resume unless you need to conserve space.

- Avoid jargon whenever possible except in an electronic resume. Your readers may not be familiar with it; furthermore, it might insult them.

- Refer to specific projects and responsibilities with words that describe measurable (quantifiable) results.

- Include information on extracurricular activities that illustrate your qualities such as leadership, teamwork, or the ability to save time or money (major concerns of all businesses).

- Write in the past tense, except for current jobs and activities.

- Skip formal wording; it may give the reader the impression that you are rigid and stuffy or, worse, pretentious.

- Give brief descriptions of any organizations or awards you have mentioned and any acronyms you have used that are not common knowledge.

NOUN FORMS (For Use in Electronic Resumes)

Accountant	Electrician	Language	Programmer	Surveyor
Administration	Electronics	Management	Publications	Teacher
Advertising	Engineer	Marketing	Public Relations	Team Leader
Analyst	Entrepreneur	Mathematics	Public Speaking	Teamwork
Animation	Experience	Manager	Purchaser	Technician
Assembly	Finances	Microprocessor	Radiology	Therapist
Award	Function	Narration	Rehabilitation	Trainer
Bookkeeper	Graphic Designer	Negotiation	Repairer	Transcription
Communication	Honors	Network	Research	Vendor
Corporate	Injection	Network Information	Sales	Writer
Customer Relations	Interface Design	Officer	Service	
Director	Internship	Operating System	Specialist	
Draftsperson	Intuition	Pathologist	Supervisor	
Editor	Investigation	Personnel	Surgery	

VERB FORMS (For Use in Printed Resumes)

Achieved	Designed	Financed	Moderated	Processed	Sorted
Administrated	Determined	Formulated	Monitored	Programmed	Succeeded
Allocated	Developed	Generated	Motivated	Promoted	Summarized
Analyzed	Diagnosed	Governed	Negotiated	Proposed	Supervised
Approved	Directed	Identified	Operated	Proved	Supplied
Arranged	Discovered	Illustrated	Ordered	Provided	Supported
Assembled	Dispensed	Implemented	Organized	Recruited	Surveyed
Assisted	Distributed	Indexed	Originated	Reduced	Systematized
Attained	Earned	Initiated	Performed	Reorganized	Tested
Compiled	Engineered	Innovated	Persuaded	Reported	Trained
Completed	Established	Installed	Piloted	Researched	Transformed
Composed	Evaluated	Integrated	Pioneered	Resolved	Troubleshot
Computed	Executed	Invented	Planned	Revised	Unified
Controlled	Expanded	Investigated	Prepared	Scheduled	Updated
Coordinated	Expedited	Led	Presented	Served	Upgraded
Created	Experienced	Maintained	Presided	Simplified	Verified
Demonstrated	Facilitated	Managed	Problem-solved	Solved	

RESUME WORKSHEET

Continue items on a separate sheet if necessary.

Name:

Address:

| | City | State | ZIP Code |

Phone

Work   Home   Cell/Pager

E-mail Address(es)

Career Objective or Position Sought (may or may not be included)

Summary of Skills

List: 1. Specific things you can do. (Refer to your functional skills list)

2. Specific equipment with which you are familiar or skilled.

3. Skills gained in employment, schooling, volunteer activities, or freelance work.

BE SPECIFIC!

Other Achievements: GPA, attendance in college (if good), awards, certificates, etc.

(continued)

RESUME WORKSHEET Continued

Education

Most recent college attended

City, State (no ZIP code)

Graduation Date

Degree received (or hours completed)

Other Schools, Colleges, Trade, Votech, Certificates, etc. (Include high school

only if you took courses that are current and relevant to your objective.)

City, State

Graduation date

Degree received or hours completed

Employment Background

Present (or most recent) Job Title

Name of Company

Location

                                                    City   State

Dates Worked

Responsibilities

Second Job Title

Name of Company

Location

                                                    City   State

Dates Worked

Responsibilities

(continued)

RESUME WORKSHEET Continued

Third Job Title _____

Name of Company _____

Location _____
                           City   State

Dates Worked _____

Responsibilities _____

_____

_____

Fourth Job Title _____

Name of Company _____

Location _____
                           City   State

Dates Worked _____

Responsibilities _____

_____

_____

Military (optional: If experience shows relevant skills, include it)

Branch of Service/Location(s) _____

_____

_____

Skills Acquired: _____

_____

_____

_____

_____

List special schools, awards, certificates, volunteer work, etc.

_____

_____

_____

Cover Letters

Despite the fact that your resume is an excellent summary of your skills and experience, it doesn't always tell prospective employers everything they need to know. Many times they have to interpret the resume to determine what they believe could be of value to their organization. The purpose of a cover letter is to assist them in this and to communicate a specific personal message about how you can be an asset to their company. It helps to generate interest in you as a prospective employee and affords you the opportunity to sell yourself. As stated earlier, not including a cover letter could be reason enough for some employers to put your resume aside. Obviously, if they receive enough resumes *with* cover letters, yours could be screened out for that alone.

During the 25-plus years I've been involved in career development, I have found that of all the paperwork associated with job searching, cover letters give job searchers the most difficulty. They get as far as the heading of the letter and just don't seem to know where to go from there. Does this sound familiar? Do you have difficulty knowing what to put in a cover letter? The general principles of writing all letters will help you. Those principles apply to cover letters as well.

The guidelines in this section will help you write a cover letter. Included are the definition of a cover letter, when to use it, instructions for writing the letter, and how to convert one letter template into all the cover letters you'll need in your job search. About now, you may be asking, "Just what *is* a cover letter?"

A cover letter is a short letter, consisting of a few paragraphs, that is attached to (covers) your resume. It identifies the position for which you are applying (if you are writing for a known opening) and directs the reader to take note of relevant items in your resume. It can also point out important strengths, skills, or experience, either to emphasize items on your resume or to add information not included in the resume. It gives you the opportunity to establish and reinforce your suitability to the job for which you are applying. Use the language common to your field to indicate your knowledge and expertise in that area. Tailor your language to your reader; in other words, if you are a graphic designer writing to another designer, you can use the trade language, but if writing to a human resources person, you may want to use everyday terms. Just don't overkill—you don't want to sound pretentious (stuffy, formal, or know-it-all). Write in a conversational tone. Contractions are used in conversation so it is acceptable to use them (albeit sparingly) as if you were speaking to the person face to face; however, always use correct grammar. In the closing of the letter, give the reader correct information about how he or she can contact you and state that you would appreciate the opportunity to meet for an interview. If you are writing to a company in a distant city to which you will be traveling, give your reader the date of your arrival and say you will call for a time that is convenient for him or her to meet with you. If possible, include a phone number in that city where you may be contacted.

When Do You Use a Cover Letter?

If you have heard that you send a cover letter only when you *mail* a resume, please forget that. A cover letter should *always* be attached to your resume. I can think of only one instance when you probably wouldn't need one: when you are handing your resume to the interviewer at the same time you are being interviewed. In this situation, you can personally explain and enhance what is on the resume, and a cover letter probably is not necessary. For all other times, whether mailing, faxing, e-mailing, or dropping off your resume, I highly recommend that you use a cover letter. Why? First, the fact that you took the time and effort to write it could make the difference between your getting an invitation to interview or being screened out. Second, its enclosure is an act of courtesy and a sign of a serious, professional approach to job searching. Finally, the cover letter affords you that extra opportunity to sell yourself to a prospective employer.

Guidelines for Constructing the Letter

The opening

If possible, always address your letter to a specific person. Your intent is to make a personal connection with the reader. Use directories, newspaper ads, locate the company's website on the Internet, or just pick up the phone and call to ask for the appropriate person's name if you don't already have it. If you are just not able to get a name, address the letter to the head of the department, the person who would be in charge of the position for which you are applying: for example, "Senior Network Administrator," "Technical Supervisor," "Manager of Administrative Support," or "Director of Nursing." Instead of the usual salutation ("Dear Mr. Jones:"), use a subject line such as "Attention: Associate Editor." *Never* address a letter to "Sir or Madam," "Hiring Executive," or "To Whom It May Concern." Address it to "Human Resources" only if you've been directed to do so. The first persons to know of openings in any department are those in charge of the department. Sometimes, human resources departments are the last to know of a job opening within their company. If they are not aware of any openings when your letter and resume reach them, they may file or ignore your paperwork.

The first paragraph

Begin your first paragraph with the purpose of the letter: *Why are you writing*? State the position for which you are applying (or, if no known opening exists, the position for which you qualify). Your opening should also include a mention of a prior conversation with the person hiring, that is if you have spoken with that person. If you are writing from a referral, tell the reader who referred you. Explain why the company is attractive to you as a potential employer, but make it brief. You can also make extra points if you quote a recent industry statistic. At the end of the first paragraph, be sure to give your reader a lead-in sentence to the next paragraph. Don't leap into the next paragraph without letting your reader know where you are going. This is called a **transitional sentence,** and it prepares the reader for what's to follow. You can see an example of a good lead-in sentence to the second paragraph in the cover letter sample in Exhibit A.13. *I am confident that upon review of my qualifications, you will find that I am a strong candidate for your next available opening.*

As my resume indicates, I have just completed a program at the American Trades Institute specializing in Heating, Ventilation, Air Conditioning, and Refrigeration. Some sample opening paragraphs appear in the box on page 68.

The second and third paragraphs

In the second and third paragraphs, state the qualifications you have for the position. Now is the time to sell yourself to the employer. Why should the employer select you to interview? Remember, you are of interest to a potential employer only because of your possible value to them, not because you want a job. Establish your value by referring to and expanding on your resume. *Relate your qualifications to their needs*. In any selling situation, you make the sale (i.e., get the job) because you find a need and fill it. To do this in your cover letter, you must first have done your research and know something about the company to which you are applying. The most valuable message you can convey to an employer is that you know the company well enough to know what its needs are and how you can help fill those needs. (See Chapter 4 to learn how to research companies.)

The closing paragraph

The last paragraph of your letter, which will be either the third or fourth, is called the **closing.** In this paragraph, thank the reader for taking the time to review your qualifications; however, do not offer thanks for anything he or she hasn't done. Doing so implies that you assume the reader is going to do it, which is insulting to the reader. *Always verify your desire for an interview;* this is the reason you are writing, isn't it? You could say something like "I would welcome the opportunity to speak with you or a designee to see if I could be of benefit to you." You may also suggest a date and a time when you are available and indicate that the interview be at the reader's convenience. If you say you are going to follow up with a call or other correspondence, make certain you do so because this could encourage the reader to wait for your call instead of contacting you. If your address or phone number has changed since you printed the resume, give the new information. Never use correction fluid or write over anything on your resume. Reprint the resume or include the information in the closing paragraph of your letter.

SAMPLE OPENING PARAGRAPHS

1. Enclosed is my application for the position of graphic arts designer for which you advertised in the *Denver Post* on Sunday, June 5, 2008.

2. Mr. Barry Elwood, my computer teacher at Westwood College of Technology, recommended I contact you about the possibility of openings for medical assistants at your clinic.

3. I read with interest your article in *Women in the Workplace,* "The Double Standard in Sexuality in American Society." I have done some extensive research on this subject and have some theories that might be of interest to you.

4. Thank you for the opportunity to discuss my qualifications with you as they relate to the sales position you have available. As we decided, I will meet with you on Tuesday, April 5, 2007, at 10 A.M. I look forward to meeting with you in person to explore further the possibility of my becoming part of your sales team.

5. I am a recent environmental science graduate of the University of Colorado in Boulder, and I am interested in employment in the San Francisco area. Because my background experience and education are focused on the current problem of toxic waste and environmental protection, I am interested in any appropriate positions with Applied Environmental, Inc.

6. While employed at Resource Data Maintenance, Inc. as a customer service engineer, I have enjoyed many opportunities to speak with some of your satisfied customers. Further investigation and research on your company has

(continued)

SAMPLE OPENING PARAGRAPHS Continued

proven to me that I would like very much to become an employee of KOP Consulting Engineers, Inc.

7. I am most interested in determining if you have any openings for an assistant general manager or manager trainee at your hotel. I would like to relocate to the Dallas area, and from my research on the Raintree Inns, I know I would like to become an employee with a well-respected establishment such as yours.

8. Enclosed is my application for the position of administrative assistant that we discussed yesterday in our phone conversation. As I mentioned, I've just completed my associate's degree in the executive secretarial program at American Career Schools here in New Rochelle, and I'm eager to apply my new skills to this position.

9. Glen Fries, production and engineering systems manager at Advanced Systems Engineering, Inc., suggested that I contact you concerning the openings you have for electronic technicians. He highly recommended your company as a leader in digital microprocessor-based circuitry, and this strongly appeals to me because I am very interested in this branch of technology.

10. In our brief conversation on the phone yesterday, you asked me to send you a resume with information about my abilities and achievements. I have enclosed a copy of my most recent resume as well as some letters of recommendation I've received from my previous employers. I believe you will find that my skills match those of your current opening for a computer programmer.

11. Please accept the enclosed resume as application for the opening you have for an automotive technician. I've been involved with the automotive industry since age 12, when I spent my evenings and Saturdays helping my dad in his automotive repair shop. Now I have my associate's degree in automotive technology from the Universal Technical Institute, and I am eager to get started on my new career.

12. Your advertisement in today's *Herald* for a vice president of marketing interests me very much. I will be graduating in June from Park University, and I am excited about the possibility of working for a firm such as yours because of the excellent reputation you have for innovative marketing techniques. Please accept the enclosed resume as application for the position of vice president of marketing.

PRINCIPLES OF COVER LETTER WRITING

- The purpose of your cover letter is to get the recipient to read your resume, to apply for a specific job (or to inquire about the possibility of employment), to arouse interest in you as a potential employee, and to ask for an interview.
- Each letter should be carefully adapted and personalized for each employer. Never reproduce a form letter and fill in the company name. Type or word-process each individual letter and sign each one by hand.
- Use a business-style format, either semiblock or block. Use the cover letter samples, Exhibits 2.9 and 2.10, as a guide or consult any good business correspondence text for instruction on letter formatting.

- Use paper that matches your resume if at all possible.
- Include information about the skills and qualifications you have that could be of interest or benefit to the employer.
- Do not mention salary requirements or past salaries unless you have been asked to do so. If asked, it is wise to give a salary range and add that you are willing to negotiate. Including past salaries could affect your ability to get the salary you deserve, especially if they were lower than what you are now qualified for. (Note: *Before entering into any discussion on salaries, consult the section on salary negotiation at the end of Chapter 5.*)
- Keep the letter to one page unless there is a valid reason. Ideally, it should contain no more than three to four paragraphs.
- Use concise, simple sentences and be especially careful to avoid sentence fragments. Avoid formal, flowery language; write in a natural, conversational tone.
- *Proofread and proofread again* for content, correct spelling, punctuation, and word usage. Ask yourself: Does the letter say what I want it to say? Is it clear and concise?
- Use this A-I-D-A checklist to make sure your letter is complete and effective:
  - **Attention:** Did you attract the reader's attention in the first paragraph sufficiently to make him or her want to read further? You can do this by informing the reader of one of your accomplishments that is relevant to the job description or advertisement, or by mentioning something you have learned about the company that excites you.
  - **Interest:** Did you point out why you would be an excellent match for the organization? Another way to spark interest is to mention personal contacts, mutual acquaintances, etc.
  - **Desire:** Have you created a desire in your reader to call you for an interview by stating examples of how you could be of benefit to the company? Give results of your achievements that would match the company's needs. Be very specific about how these relate to the job. Now is the time to use the benefit statements you wrote in the first section.
  - **Action:** Did you ask for the interview? Did you suggest a time? Did you supply information about how to contact you?

How to Create All Your Cover Letters from One Letter

Once you've composed a basic cover letter template, you can modify it and use it again and again. Simply change the first paragraph to indicate the person's name to whom you are writing, the position that interests you, and information about the company. In the second and third paragraphs, focus on your skills and qualifications relevant to this specific position and company. To sell yourself to this particular company, list your qualifications, experience, or education (which may or may not be on your resume).

To see how a cover letter can be modified, study the two cover letters from John Jones (see Exhibits 2.9 and 2.10). You may also use the sample opening paragraphs in the previous box as a guide to how opening paragraphs change to adapt to the writer's intent. With these guides, you should have no difficulty in writing any cover letter that you'll need. Of course, don't hesitate to use your own creativity. (See Exhibits A.11 through A.20 in the appendix for more sample letters.)

EXHIBIT 2.9 Sample cover letter.

11567 East 17th Street
Spokane, WA 01435
September 2, 2008

Mr. Kevin Schultz
ABC Data Processing
3498 South Ivy Way
Suite 1160
Spokane, WA 01437

Dear Mr. Schultz:

Jane Hill, Student Services Director at Spokane Technical Institute, recommended
ABC Data Processing as an excellent company to work for because of its reputation for total commitment to its employees' growth and advancement. My own
research of your company indicates that it is the kind of progressive company
I would like to work for.

My experience and education are summarized for you on the enclosed resume.
Not mentioned there is a computer operations and programming internship that
I participated in while attending classes at STI. The internship took place at the
Regional Transportation District, where I gained experience with Java, Pert, and
C++. I believe that my experience and education qualify me to work effectively
and productively in your department. I could contribute to the goals of ABC
Data Processing as I learn new concepts and ideas quickly, and this would save
you time and money in that I would require a shorter training period.

I would like to meet with you to discuss employment requirements and opportunities at ABC Data Processing. I look forward to hearing from you soon with
reference to a possible future with your company.

Sincerely,

John E. Jones

John E. Jones
(509) 555-4587
johnjones95@aol.com

Enclosure: Resume

11567 East 17th Street
Spokane, WA 01435
September 16, 2007

Ms. Elaine Calovet
Data Processing Manager
Seattle Medical Manufacturers
170 Denny Way
Seattle, WA 01539

Dear Ms. Calovet:

I enjoyed speaking with you on the phone yesterday and learning of the computer operations position that is available with Seattle Medical Manufacturers. I look forward to the opportunity to interview with you for this position.

If you will review the enclosed resume, you will see that I have experience in computer computations and data processing in addition to the education I've received at Spokane Technical Institute. The training there was in a work-simulated environment and consisted primarily of hands-on self-instruction. I believe that my education, coupled with an internship at the Regional Transportation District, qualifies me for this position. In the internship, I gained experience with Java, Pert, and C++.

I would very much appreciate an interview with you to discuss how my qualifications could serve as an asset to Seattle Medical Manufacturers. You may contact me at the number below or leave a message (I have voice messaging), and I will return your call as soon as I return. You may also contact me at my e-mail address: johnjones95@aol.com.

Thank you for taking the time to consider my application for the position of computer operator with your company.

Sincerely,

John E. Jones

John E. Jones
(509) 555-4587
johnjones95@aol.com

Enclosure: Resume, reference letters

LETTER STRUCTURE

Correct letter structure is important to any effective business correspondence. If you use an accepted format, your letter will be easier to read and understand. Every letter, formal or informal, contains a *heading,* a *salutation,* a *body,* and a *closing.* (See Letter Structure sample on page 74.)

HEADING

- In a business letter, this is your company's name and address. In a personal letter, or if you are not representing a company, this is your own address.
- The date.
- Name, title, and address of the person receiving the letter. Be sure to spell the name of the recipient correctly and use his or her correct title (if known).

SALUTATION

The salutation follows the inside address. A formal one is preferred for business letters unless you know the person very well.

BODY

The body of the letter contains your message and request for action. It is organized into three sections: introduction, main body, and conclusion.

- *Introduction:* The first sentence of the letter lets your reader know why you are writing, the purpose of the letter.
- *Main body:* The main body of the letter presents your message in organized, easily understood paragraphs. In a cover letter, it should contain no more than one or two paragraphs.
- *Conclusion:* In a cover letter, the conclusion should thank the reader for taking the time to consider your qualifications and end with asking for an invitation to interview. Always end your letter on a positive note.

CLOSING

All letters end with a complimentary close and your signature above your typed name. Accepted closings for business letters are:

Yours truly,   Sincerely,

Yours very truly,   Sincerely yours,

The closing used most often for cover letters is "Sincerely." After the complimentary closing, type your name and title (if you have one) four lines down from the close, and always sign your name above. It is also a good practice in cover letters to include your phone number and e-mail address after your typed name. (See cover letter samples A.12 to A.20 in the appendix.)

COVER LETTER FORMAT (Semiblock Style, Standard Punctuation)

5101 Cherry Twig Road   *RETURN*
Omaha, NE 68835   *ADDRESS*
October 25, 2008   *DATELINE*

4 lines

Mr. Randolf Manning
Omaha Central Power Supply   *INSIDE ADDRESS*
P.O. Box 32789
Omaha, NE 68746
    Line space
Dear Mr. Manning: *SALUTATION*
    Line space
Please accept this letter and the enclosed resume as application for the position of Systems Analyst that you advertised in the *Omaha World Herald* on October 23, 2008. I am very interested in having an opportunity to apply my knowledge and background experience to program analysis, as well as put to use my fascination for the field of energy, to the continued success of Omaha Central Power Supply.
    Line space
As you can see from my resume, I have a solid background in the field. My qualifications include training and experience as a programmer with skill application in program modification and design. I also have had some association with documentation and recommendations for program improvement methods. I believe that I fulfill the requirements of this position and will be an asset to your department.
    Line space
I am a dedicated and loyal person as is demonstrated by my ten years of employment where I advanced to Chief Design Programmer at The Sterling Company in Lincoln. I believe in the old-fashioned work ethic and am committed to above-average job performance. I know I could save Omaha Central Power Supply time and money by implementing a program design Ive developed that reduces energy costs by 25%.
    Line space
Thank you for taking the time to consider my qualifications as they pertain to the goals of Omaha Central Power Supply. I look forward to meeting with you at your earliest convenience.
    Line space

Sincerely,   *COMPLIMENTARY CLOSE*

Cheryl Kowalski   *WRITER'S NAME*
(308) 555-1462
ckowalski@gpcom.net

    Line space
ENCLOSURE NOTATION

Follow-Up Letters

Many job seekers breathe a sigh of relief after they've completed their resume and cover letter, thinking they are finally finished with the paperwork. Not so, if you want a final, professional touch to your job searching efforts. There are always follow-up letters to write. A note thanking the interviewer for his or her time, a letter to cultivate future job offers when you weren't granted an interview, a resurrection letter to remind an employer of your application, or a letter to refuse a job offer are all important parts of successful follow-up. Unfortunately, only about 10 percent of the people looking for jobs bother to send them.

Sending a thank-you letter actually could be the determining factor in being selected over another applicant, all other things being equal, of course. Some interviewers consider this a vital part of the hiring process. It is a necessary step. To see why, imagine that an employer has interviewed all the applicants and is down to deciding between two candidates. They have equal qualifications, they both interviewed well, and both have a personality that the interviewer believes will fit with the organization. One applicant sends a short note thanking the interviewer, and the other applicant does not. If you were the interviewer, which applicant would you be more likely to choose?

A thank-you letter is short and concise, no more than two brief paragraphs. Should you type it or handwrite it? Experts disagree. Letitia Baldridge, well-known expert on professional manners, advises using the computer's word processor and using nice stationery, following the same principles as you would for any correspondence. I agree that you should follow good correspondence protocol; however, I suggest handwriting your thank-you on simple note stationery. A handwritten note adds a personal touch. If you were in the place of the interviewer, when you pick up your mail, which envelope would you open first—the one that is standard business size, or the one that is greeting-card size? Note cards are inexpensive and can be purchased at department, stationery, or discount stores.

Always send a thank-you letter after *every interview*, and send one to each individual interviewer, not one for all of them. Also, it's a good selling point to send one to others in the company who have helped you. Whether you type it or handwrite it is certainly your option.

What does a thank-you letter say? First, that you appreciate the time the interviewer spent with you. Second, it should state you are impressed with the company and why. Third, it must tell the reader that you really want the job (if you do), reiterating how your qualifications match those discussed in the interview. Something you can do to help clinch the interviewer's interest in you is to mention some problem the interviewer discussed during the interview and suggest a possible solution or strategy for resolving it. By the way, this is also an opportune time to add anything you forgot to say in the interview or to ask questions you neglected to ask.

When should you send it? Within five to seven days? No—sit down immediately after the interview and mail it that day. If you know they are making a decision that evening, you should e-mail one and follow up with a hard copy. You want it to arrive before the decision to hire is made and while the interviewer still remembers who you are. Faces and personalities tend to fade very quickly, especially when the interviewer is seeing a lot of applicants.

If you are declining a job offer, give the reason for declining and, as in the thank-you letter, thank the interviewer for the time and interest in you. Sometime in the future, that company may have an opening that interests you. If you've left the firm with a favorable image of you, it will be more likely to contact you about the new position.

SAMPLE THANK-YOU LETTERS

Dear Mr./Ms. _____:

Thank you for your interest in me as a possible applicant for the position of _____ with (company name).

I enjoyed meeting with you and am very interested in becoming an employee of your company. I was impressed with the state-of-the-art computer equipment and software programs you are using.

I wish you continued success and look forward to hearing from you.

Sincerely,

Dear Mr./Ms._____:

I appreciate the opportunity I had to interview with you for the position of _____ on ___(date)___. I was very interested to learn that you are using Adobe In Design 2.0 and Corel Painter 8 because they are my favorites. I believe that my experience with Corel, Adobe, and PhotoShop, in addition to my other administrative skills, would enable me to be an asset to ___(name of company)___.

Thank you again for your time and your interest in me as a potential employee of your company. I would very much like to fill your opening for ___(name of company)___.

Sincerely,

Dear Mr./Ms._____:

Thank you for such an interesting and informative interview yesterday. I was extremely impressed with the emphasis you place on customer and employee satisfaction. My observation while there yesterday confirmed my research on ___(name of company)___, that you do, in fact, genuinely care about your personnel.

I am excited about the possibility of becoming a member of your team. If you need any further information, you may contact me at (444) 333-4444 from 8:30 A.M. until 5:30 P.M. or in the evenings at (444) 222-1111. I look forward to hearing from you.

Yours truly,

Another time to write a follow-up letter is when you have submitted a resume to inquire about the possibility of openings or to apply for a known opening and have received a reply such as "We're sorry, but . . . we'll keep your resume on file"; in such cases, it is to your benefit to write a brief letter of thanks to the person for taking the time to review your qualifications. You do this for the reason already mentioned: You want to be considered for future openings.

The Application for Employment

More paperwork! During your job search, you will probably fill out many employment applications. The importance of this part of the paperwork is not to be minimized; employers also use this document as a screening device. If they see a half-completed, sloppily written application, they assume the person who completed it is also sloppy and careless. Job seekers tend not to understand that if a job application is not filled out correctly and completely, it could cost them an interview, or worse, a job offer.

Employers design applications to give them specific information relative to their organizations, items you might not have included in your resume or cover letter. One absolute is never to write on the application "See resume." Do not put this anywhere on an application form; it is viewed as lazy and disrespectful. The saying is true: "Resumes tell the employers what *you* want them to know, and job applications tell them what *they* want to know."

Now it is reality time. You're facing a form that is asking for your life history, to account for every breath of your life since puberty, and you are not given very much space to do it. Heaven forbid that you now have to reveal yourself. I really believe this is the reason we all hate forms: the lack of space to write in and the darn things want us to "tell all." So you hurry through it, just wanting to get it over with and sometimes making fatal mistakes. You needn't suffer from "application phobia"—there is a painless and correct way to complete them. To help ensure that yours will be among the best that the employer sees, observe the following guidelines carefully.

- If possible, obtain an application form before going to the interview. If you can get one, fill it out in your own time, making sure you have all your information correct. Then you can take it with you when you go to the interview. When you do have to fill out one in the employer's office before the interview, if you make an error, ask for another form. Erasures and correction fluid are usually not viewed favorably. Whatever you do, do not turn an application in with scratched-out words.

- Always take two or three pens with you to an interview. Try them out at home to make sure that they don't bleed or drop spots of ink. Always use black ink pens because blue does not reproduce well on most fax machines and some copy machines. Also, this is a legal document and should be filled out in black ink. Of course, any other colors, such as red, purple, or pink, are totally unacceptable.

- Have the necessary information with you. Never ask for a telephone directory to look up addresses and numbers; this is the ultimate sign of unpreparedness. You can use the resume worksheets in this book for this information.

- Read the entire application through before beginning, and then reread each question before you begin writing to make certain you understand what the question is asking for. Filling out application forms resembles taking a test (actually, it is your first test with this employer). More mistakes are made from not reading carefully than from any other reason. One employer says that if he sees a sloppily filled out application form, that applicant has just failed the first test, and he will not hire that applicant no matter what the other qualifications are. This was an employer at a company where the employees had to complete daily service orders.

- If you need a dictionary to check terms and spelling, use one. Have one with you so you don't risk errors in grammar or spelling or in the use of technical terms. The term *technician* is misspelled more times than you might believe. Technical terms and jargon are especially tricky, so make certain you use and spell them correctly.

- Never leave anything blank. If you don't understand what a question is asking for, find out. If it doesn't apply to you, write "NA" (not applicable) in the space. If you leave it blank, the reader has no way of knowing whether you carelessly missed it or just didn't want to answer it.

- For open-ended questions, such as those that ask for an opinion, organize your thoughts carefully and write them on a separate piece of paper before transferring your response to the form.

- Always include a phone number where you can be contacted if you do not have voice mail or an answering machine. And give your e-mail address if you have one because today so many people are communicating in that manner. Remember, a missed call might mean a missed interview or job offer.

- When you go to fill out an application form at the employer's place of business, take the following with you: social security card, a small dictionary, grade transcripts, any certificates or documents that you would need for verification of data, and all your history information, including a list of references.

- When you finish, go back over the form and double-check for errors or anything you might have missed.

Troublesome Areas

When I teach classes on the paperwork of job searching and we get to the session on employment applications, the questions I encounter most often are about legal and illegal questions. Another common concern is how to complete the "Reason for Leaving" line in the work experience section. Finally, applicants ask what they should put in the salary requirement blank. Let's tackle these questions first.

Illegal questions

If I told you you would never encounter any illegal questions, I would be lying. I have seen application forms that left me appalled at the obvious ignorance of the employer. If you are given an application with illegal questions on issues such as age, marital status, religion, or race, you may wish to write "NA" (not applicable) in the blank. You certainly do not have to answer them. (If they are on a separate page that states the questions are for the company's affirmative action program, the information should not be used in the hiring process. Whether to answer them is your choice.) Believe it or not, some employers are not aware of the questions on their application forms, and many are ignorant of the legalities in the hiring process. If an employer is asking illegal questions on the form or in the interview, you probably should ask yourself, "Do I want to work for someone like this?" It's your call.

Reason for leaving

If you are afraid to explain why you left a job because you were fired or asked to resign for other than favorable reasons, don't worry. You do not have to state the reason on the application. There are ways to answer without hurting your chances. First, you need to know that being fired is not usually a reason employers choose not to hire someone; it is how you handle the question in the interview that could disqualify you. Instead of writing that you were fired, you can write you would like to discuss this in the interview. At that time, you have the opportunity to explain the circumstances surrounding the termination. For how to explain this during the interview, refer to the section titled "Questions You Could Be Asked and How to Answer" in Chapter 4.

Salary requirement

Another area on employment applications that causes applicants to eliminate themselves unknowingly is the inquiry about salary requirements. This is an important but also sensitive factor in the job search process that needs to be handled carefully. If you have done the necessary research, you know what is an appropriate range for you and also have some idea of the salary this company is willing to pay. You can acquire this information about salary ranges from many sources, such as informational interviews (discussed in Chapter 3), magazines and newspapers that publish special sections throughout the year, directories in the library, college placement offices, the Internet, and people you know who are already working in the field. The best answer is to state a range (yearly, monthly, or hourly) and always add that it is negotiable. If you give a figure that is too low, an employer will most likely be delighted to give it to you. Employers have a commitment to make a profit, and they will hire you as economically as they can. However, if you set a figure or range too high, the employer might assume that you are out of reach. So do your homework and know the range that is appropriate for you.

If you complete the application according to these suggestions, you will present yourself to the interviewer as a conscientious and thorough person who is serious about his or her job search. It will also give you an edge over other applicants who have not done their homework. To practice and prepare yourself for filling out employers' application forms, complete the sample form in Exhibit 2.11.

Application for employment.   **EXHIBIT 2.11**

APPLICATION FOR EMPLOYMENT

PRE-EMPLOYMENT
QUESTIONNAIRE
AN EQUAL
OPPORTUNITY EMPLOYER

LAST

PERSONAL INFORMATION

NAME (LAST NAME FIRST)			SOCIAL SECURITY NO.	
PRESENT ADDRESS	APT. NO.	CITY	STATE	ZIP
PERMANENT ADDRESS	APT. NO.	CITY	STATE	ZIP

ARE YOU 18 YEARS OR OLDER? ☐ YES ☐ NO   PHONE

FIRST

DESIRED EMPLOYMENT

POSITION	DATE YOU CAN START	SALARY DESIRED

ARE YOU EMPLOYED NOW? ☐ YES ☐ NO   IF SO MAY WE INQUIRE OF YOUR PRESENT EMPLOYER? ☐ YES ☐ NO

EVER APPLIED TO THIS COMPANY BEFORE? ☐ YES ☐ NO	WHERE?	WHEN?
EVER WORKED FOR THIS COMPANY BEFORE? ☐ YES ☐ NO	WHERE?	WHEN?

REASON FOR LEAVING

NAME OF LAST SUPERVISOR AT THIS COMPANY

WHO REFERRED YOU TO THIS COMPANY?
☐ EMPLOYMENT AGENCY   ☐ NEWSPAPER ADVERTISING   ☐ FRIEND

☐ STATE EMPLOYMENT OFFICE   ☐ COLLEGE PLACEMENT SERVICE   ☐ WALK IN   ☐ OTHER

MIDDLE

EDUCATION

SCHOOL LEVEL	NAME AND LOCATION OF SCHOOL	NO. OF YEARS ATTENDED	DID YOU GRADUATE?	SUBJECTS STUDIED
GRAMMAR SCHOOL				
HIGH SCHOOL				
COLLEGE				
TRADE, BUSINESS OR CORRESPONDENCE SCHOOL				

GENERAL

SUBJECTS OF SPECIAL STUDY OR RESEARCH WORK

SPECIAL TRAINING

SPECIAL SKILLS

EXHIBIT 2.11 Continued

FORMER EMPLOYERS

LIST BELOW LAST THREE EMPLOYERS, STARTING WITH THE MOST RECENT ONE FIRST.

NAME OF PRESENT OR LAST EMPLOYER				
ADDRESS		CITY	STATE	ZIP
STARTING DATE	LEAVING DATE		JOB TITLE	
WEEKLY STARTING SALARY	WEEKLY FINAL SALARY	MAY WE CONTACT YOUR SUPERVISOR? ☐ YES ☐ NO		
NAME OF SUPERVISOR		TITLE		PHONE
DESCRIPTION OF WORK				
REASON FOR LEAVING				

NAME OF PREVIOUS EMPLOYER				
ADDRESS		CITY	STATE	ZIP
STARTING DATE	LEAVING DATE		JOB TITLE	
WEEKLY STARTING SALARY	WEEKLY FINAL SALARY	MAY WE CONTACT YOUR SUPERVISOR? ☐ YES ☐ NO		
NAME OF SUPERVISOR		TITLE		PHONE
DESCRIPTION OF WORK				
REASON FOR LEAVING				

NAME OF PREVIOUS EMPLOYER				
ADDRESS		CITY	STATE	ZIP
STARTING DATE	LEAVING DATE		JOB TITLE	
WEEKLY STARTING SALARY	WEEKLY FINAL SALARY	MAY WE CONTACT YOUR SUPERVISOR? ☐ YES ☐ NO		
NAME OF SUPERVISOR		TITLE		PHONE
DESCRIPTION OF WORK				
REASON FOR LEAVING				

(continued)

Continued　　　　　　　　　　　　　　　　　　**EXHIBIT 2.11**

REFERENCES

BELOW, GIVE THE NAMES OF THREE PERSONS YOU ARE NOT RELATED TO, WHOM YOU HAVE KNOWN AT LEAST ONE YEAR.

	NAME	ADDRESS	BUSINESS	YEARS ACQUAINTED
1				
2				
3				

SERVICE RECORD

BRANCH OF SERVICE	DISCHARGE DATE RANK

HAVE YOU BEEN CONVICTED OF A FELONY WITHIN THE LAST 5 YEARS?　☐ YES　☐ NO

IF YES, EXPLAIN. (WILL NOT NECESSARILY EXCLUDE YOU FROM CONSIDERATION)

AUTHORIZATION

"I CERTIFY THAT THE FACTS CONTAINED IN THIS APPLICATION ARE TRUE AND COMPLETE TO THE BEST OF MY KNOWLEDGE AND UNDERSTAND THAT, IF EMPLOYED, FALSIFIED STATEMENTS ON THIS APPLICATION SHALL BE GROUNDS FOR DISMISSAL.

I AUTHORIZE INVESTIGATION OF ALL STATEMENTS CONTAINED HEREIN AND THE REFERENCES AND EMPLOYERS LISTED ABOVE TO GIVE YOU ANY AND ALL INFORMATION CONCERNING MY PREVIOUS EMPLOYMENT AND ANY PERTINENT INFORMATION THEY MAY HAVE, PERSONAL OR OTHERWISE AND RELEASE THE COMPANY FROM ALL LIABILITY FOR ANY DAMAGE THAT MAY RESULT FROM UTILIZATION OF SUCH INFORMATION.

I ALSO UNDERSTAND AND AGREE THAT NO REPRESENTATIVE OF THE COMPANY HAS ANY AUTHORITY TO ENTER INTO ANY AGREEMENT FOR EMPLOYMENT FOR ANY SPECIFIED PERIOD OF TIME, OR TO MAKE ANY AGREEMENT CONTRARY TO THE FOREGOING, UNLESS IT IS IN WRITING AND SIGNED BY AN AUTHORIZED COMPANY REPRESENTATIVE."

DATE　　　　　　　　　SIGNATURE

NOTES

1. Kenneth Terrell, "When Experience Counts, Older Workers Are Finding a Welcome in the Job Market," *U.S. News and World Report,*" March 20, 2007, 48. Copyright U.S. News & World Report, L.P. Reprinted by permission.

2. For some valid information on older workers in the workplace and a list of the best employers for workers over 50, refer to the *AARP Magazine* (November/ December 2003): 51–55.

3. Joe Turner, Video Resumes, www.jobchangesecrets.com. Accessed July 6, 2007.

4. Liz Pullman Weston, "How Bad Credit Can Cost you a Job." Your Money Message Board, February 7, 2004.

5. "A Bull Market in Inflated Resumes," *U.S. News & World Report,* November 13, 2000, 78. Copyright U.S. News and World Report, L.P. Reprinted by permission.

6. Mary B. Nemnich and Fred E. Jandt, *Cyberspace Job Search Kit 2001–2002 Edition, The Complete Guide to Online Job Seeking and Career Information* (Indianapolis, IN: JIST Publishing, 2001), 94–109. Reprinted by permission.

7. Ibid.

8. Ibid.

Organizing and Planning

Now that you're inventoried and you've prepared a resume and cover letter, you are ready to begin your search for information, leads, and bona fide job openings. The first step is to organize your search. You need to learn the specific requirements for the job(s) you are targeting, discover where the jobs are, and decide how you can best use your time while you are searching. The time that it took to find a new job expanded from 2.7 months in 2006 to 3.6 months in 2007.[1] So you can safely count on your search taking that much time or longer depending on the market at the time you are searching.

3

C H A P T E R

In this chapter, we look at one of the best known ways to get information on companies, job titles, and job definitions and describe sources for leads to jobs, including those in the mysterious "hidden job market" by conducting some informational interviews and preparing a Job Skills Portfolio. In the second step of organizing, you will also learn ways to systematize and manage your time during the job search to maximize your efforts for the greatest success and the least possible stress.

Organizing

Where Do You Begin?

To begin organizing your job search, you need a list of companies in your targeted industry and some information on occupational titles and definitions. Without this information, you will most likely waste your time going off in all directions, totally unorganized, unprepared, and unproductive. So your first assignment in organizing the search is to prepare a list of the companies for which you would like to work and to get information on job titles and their definitions. This kind of information can be found in the library and on the Internet. Your local library is a good place to start. Books on organizations are classified by industry, size, and location, so you can go directly to the ones that will give you the information you need. Look for directories, trade publications, and even the yellow pages. Local newspapers and magazines are also very good sources of information on companies in your area. Here is a list of some of the many sources available to you at the library and on the Internet.

- Fitch Corporations manuals
- *Standard & Poor's Register of Corporations*
- *The Wall Street Journal*—world's leading business publication
- *Job Seeker's Guide to Private & Public Companies*—listed by location (e.g., South, North, etc.) (very expensive to buy)
- *Thomas Register of American Manufacturers*
- Dun & Bradstreet's *Reference Book*
- College Placement Annuals
- *The Best Hospitals in America*—check for listings in *U.S. News & World Report*
- Moody's Manuals
- MacRae's Bluebook
- *Travel & Hospitality Career Directory*
- *Therapists and Allied Health Professionals Directory*—gives career options
- *Applied Science & Technology Index*—indexes 400 trade magazines and industry and scholarly publications
- *BusinessWeek*—updated company profiles
- *U.S. News & World Report*
- *Business Periodicals Index*—covers general business periodicals and trade journals

- *Directory of Corporate Affiliations*—has links to global company directory
- *Directory of American Research & Technology*—has links to many fields
- *U. S. Government Manual*—free as an electronic publication
- National Trade & Professional Associations of U.S.—lists 17,000+ associations and 26,000+ executives
- Data Processing Management Association—has link for data processing job opportunities

The library and the Internet also have two publications that cover career information and jobs: the *Occupational Outlook Handbook* (*OOH*, a classic reference about occupations from A to Z; (use the search box for specific topics) and the *Dictionary of Occupational Titles* (*DOT*). The *Occupational Outlook Handbook* describes what workers do on the job, working conditions, the training and education needed, earnings, and the expected job prospects in a wide range of occupations. The *DOT* contains definitions for nearly 13,000 job "codes" and encompasses approximately 20,000 job titles and nearly 13,000 detailed definitions. If you need help in locating information about the occupation that interests you, ask the librarian.

The Internet offers a wealth of information about companies. To learn about companies, visit the sites of the sources just listed. Don't forget to check magazines and newspapers. For information about jobs, you can go to the *DOT* online at www.wave.net/upg/immigration/dot_index.html or the *OOH* at www.bls.gov/oco. On the *OOH* site, to find information by occupation, enter the name of your specific occupation in the box labeled "Search by occupation." If you would like to see a listing of all occupations, click the A–Z button.

As you find information at the library and on the Internet, build a comprehensive list of names of companies and be sure to record exactly where you got the name of the company. If you find later that you want to go back and get more information, nothing is more frustrating than to have to try to remember which directory, publication, and so on, listed that company. Once you have compiled a list of the companies you are interested in (depending on your field, you should have at least 20 to 50 names), you are now ready for the next step in organizing your job search, the *informational interview*.

The Informational Interview

It has been said that if you want to find out how to get where you want to go, talk to someone who's already there. That is exactly what informational interviews are for. The one sure way to find out if your skills and abilities match your targeted job is by talking to those working in your field. You can find out all about the characteristics and requirements of the position, plus many tips for success and insight into the future of your field. An informational interview can eliminate surprises in the job interview and give you some intelligent questions and answers for your interviewer. Moreover, informational interviews can help you develop employment leads and gain experience with interviewing. It is not unusual for informational interviews to lead to job offers.

Strategies for Conducting an Informational Interview

Choose the top-five companies from your list

Not all of the companies you call will have someone available to meet with you, so choose the top five from your list and work down from there.

Plan your call

Before you pick up the phone, you must plan your call. You don't want to waste the person's time or risk sounding like you're unprepared. Write out what you're going to say and then practice it. Your conversation should not sound canned, but you do want to sound professional.

Get to the person in charge of the department for the type of job you are targeting

The person who answers the phone is usually a receptionist or a secretary who has been trained to screen calls; therefore, you must be prepared to handle the person's attempt to screen you out. Be firm but polite, and state that this is *not* an employment call, but an information call. Stress that you are not looking for work at this time; you simply would like to learn more about the field and would appreciate speaking with someone who has that information. If the employee is reluctant to transfer your call and puts you off by saying that the person you want to speak to is "out," "in a meeting," or "on the phone," *get a name* and call back and ask for that person directly. If the employee asks you to leave your name and number, *don't.* The chance that you will receive a return call is next to none. Just say that you are going to be away from your phone and you'd like to try again, and ask what would be a good time to call.

Identify yourself and state the purpose of your call

When you have been connected to the person you wish to talk to, don't waste that person's time. Be prepared and explain immediately who you are and why you are calling. Be sure to emphasize that you need his or her expertise; this is one of the highest compliments you can pay anyone and should help you to gain an interview. It's true; you *do* need that individual's expertise. Ask for a few (15 to 20) minutes of time when it is convenient for him or her to meet with you. Some busy people may try to conduct this interview over the phone; therefore, you must stress that you are very interested in observing just how the job is performed and would learn much more by visiting in person. Once you have confirmed a date and a time, ask if there is anything you need to know about the location, restrictions on parking, or entry into the company. Some computer companies and government organizations have security measures to protect their operations. *Write down all of this information; do not trust it to memory.* (See the techniques and tips for using the telephone for job and interview calls at the end of this section.)

Prepare your questions

Part of the preparation for an informational interview is to decide on the kinds of questions you are going to ask in the interview. What is it that you would like to know? What kinds of things are pertinent and appropriate to ask? The objective of your interview is to find out all you can about the requirements and characteristics of the job you are looking for and your industry. To help you stay on target and not waste your time and that of the interviewee, either choose questions from the list here or make up your own. Remember, you are asking questions related to information, not to get a job at that time. This frees you up to ask questions that would not be appropriate in an interview, such as numbers 1,2,4, and 11. If you were interviewing for a job and had done the necessary research, you should already know the answers to these questions.

SAMPLE QUESTIONS

1. What does the company do?
2. How old is the company; how long has it been in business?
3. Where are its plants, stores, locations?
4. What are its products or services?
5. Who are its competitors?
6. In each major division, what types of positions are offered?
7. What are the requirements for entry-level and experienced positions (education, skills, abilities, etc.)?
8. What are the main duties and responsibilities of the job?
9. Where is the job performed (indoors, outdoors, travel)?
10. What personal qualities does the company look for?
11. Is any certification or licensing required to be eligible for hire?
12. What, if any, are the tools, equipment, software, computer languages, experience, and so on, needed to perform the job?
13. What are the opportunities for advanced training, on-the-job training, or academic coursework? Is this paid for by the firm?
14. What is the salary range? What could one expect to make five years from now?
15. What benefits are provided by the company?
16. What does the interviewee see as the future of this occupation? Will there be an increase or a decrease in demand for it? What are you plans for growth in this industry?`
17. What changes could arise in this position or field over the next few years? How could you prepare for these changes?
18. How much involvement do employees have in decision making and policy making?
19. What other companies might employ individuals wishing to enter your field?
20. Could the interviewee suggest any other people you could talk to for more information about opportunities in your field?

Conduct the interview professionally

Bring your questions with you to the interview and use them as guidelines to keep you from straying from your objective, which is to get information. Treat this interview as seriously as you would an actual job interview: Dress professionally, be on time, listen carefully, and make good eye contact during the interview. *If you have cleared it with the person you are interviewing*, you might want to bring a tape recorder because it will allow you to be more relaxed and not have to concentrate on taking notes during the interview. Keep to the allotted time unless the person you're interviewing willingly offers more. When the interview is over, always thank the person for spending time with you, and don't forget to ask for referrals.

Follow up

There is only one way to follow up an information interview: with a thank-you note. Writing the thank-you is a professional courtesy. All you need to say is that you really appreciate the time the person took from a busy day to spend with you and how much it has helped you in your research. Send the thank-you as soon as possible after the interview. If other people helped you to arrange the interview, write to them as well.

Caution: Don't take your resume to informational interviews. I hear lots of objections from people about this, such as "But what if they offer me a job or ask for my resume, shouldn't I take it with me?" Well, what did you tell the interviewee that you were there for? Was it for getting a job or for getting information? Do you want the interviewee to think you had ulterior motives, that you're not honest? Besides, not having your resume with you gives you the opportunity to offer to bring it by later and maybe get a job interview at the same time.

Making Calls for Information and Job Openings

The telephone is one of the best tools available to you when job searching. Whether you use it to arrange for informational interviews or to locate job openings, it is the swiftest way to contact prospective employers. However, to avoid wasting the time of the person you are calling, or worse, losing a possible job opening, you must be prepared. You need to be clear about your objective (the reason you are calling) and have a well-thought-out plan that includes a prepared phone script.

Your Objective

If you are calling for an informational interview, your objective is to speak with the person who is qualified to give you the information you're seeking and to grant you an interview. If you are calling about job openings, your objective is to get to the person who knows firsthand about those openings. If you are calling from an advertised opening or referral, you will probably have been directed to ask for a certain person; when you reach that person, begin by asking for an interview.

Planning Your Call

A receptionist or secretary will probably answer your call; therefore, your first strategy should be to obtain the name of the person with whom you wish to speak (unless you already know it). Keep in mind that secretaries and receptionists have often been trained to "protect" their superiors from unnecessary calls and might not readily give out their names. What you say at this time can be crucial. It is always best to ask for the person in charge of the department that you are interested in, *not* the person in charge of hiring. You may be asked if this is an employment call. If it is, say so. If the reply is "I'm sorry, but we're not hiring at this time," or "We have no openings at this time," simply say, "But if you were hiring, to whom would I speak?" Once you have a name, thank the employee, hang up, and call back later asking for that person.

If the receptionist or secretary refers you to someone in the personnel department, go ahead and speak with that person. However, avoid personnel people if at all possible because they are usually the last ones to know about openings and many times will screen you out based on preset guidelines. Instead, you want the opportunity to sell yourself to the person who is qualified to judge whether or not you could be of use to the company.

If you are successful in getting the name of the person who is in charge of the area you're interested in but are told that that person is out or in a meeting, don't leave your name and number. Just say you are going to be in and out and that you will call back.

Whatever the result is in your dealings with receptionists or secretaries, always remember this: Treat them with respect and courtesy. Not only is this the right thing to do in dealing with anyone, but you also want them to be on your side. They can be very helpful should there be an opening. They can help you arrange an interview, and they often have a say in who gets hired.

Your Telephone Script

Once you've been connected to the person you wish to speak with, your call should be brief and to the point. Whatever the reason you are calling, whether for a job opening or information, begin by telling the person who you are and the purpose of your call.

For information: "Good (morning, afternoon), my name is John Smith, and I am interested in learning about the field of (information technology auditing, computer networking, drafting, engineering, hospitality, medicine, etc.) and about career opportunities in this field."

For job leads: "Good (morning, afternoon), my name is Mary Jones, and I'm interested in any openings you have in _____. I'm a recent graduate of (name of college) with a/an (associate's, bachelor's, master's) degree in _____."

If you are calling to inquire about job openings, after your introduction, be prepared to offer some strong selling points for meeting with you. Mention special skills, experience, and abilities. Have your resume and/or portfolio handy, and use it to summarize your strongest qualifications for the position. Be brief but assertive, and describe why your abilities would be of value to the company.

The Close: Get the interview!

This is the objective of your call; don't lose sight of it. If this is a job call, now is the time to remember that you are not asking for a handout, you are offering something of value, an opportunity for the employer to hire a dedicated, hardworking, and valuable employee—you! A closing statement to help you get an interview might be "I would really appreciate the opportunity to meet with you to discuss my qualifications as they relate to the opening in _____. I have tomorrow morning or anytime on Tuesday free; which is most convenient for you?"

ADDITIONAL TIPS FOR SUCCESSFUL COLD CALLS

- Be enthusiastic, smile, and project a positive attitude. Even though the other person can't see you, your attitude and the way you feel projects over the phone.

- Make your calls in a quiet place without distractions from children, pets, or roommates.

- Have all your paperwork in front of you: script, resume, daily planner, whatever other information you need.

- Choose the best time to call. Anytime after 9 A.M., even during lunch hours, is a good time to call. In some small- to medium-size companies, managers and even owners cover the phones while the receptionist is out to lunch. After 3 P.M. can also be an opportune time to call because it's usually a less busy time of day. Friday afternoons may also be good because people are looking forward to the weekend and are in a good mood. Avoid calling on Monday morning or before 9 o'clock on any day. Most businesspeople like that time to be uninterrupted by phone calls.

- Be prepared for rejection. Keep in mind that a "no" is not about you personally. Making job calls and looking for openings is a numbers game. The law of averages says that after a certain number of no's, it is inevitable that a yes will follow. That's Murphy's law. Just keep calling; be persistent!

- Always get all the information you need for follow-up, interviews, and so on, and *write it down*!

- If you have voice mail or an answering machine, always record a simple, but professional, message. A caller could be offended by an unprofessional message.

Job Skills Portfolio

The next step after you've completed your informational interviewing and have knowledge of the skills and abilities that employers desire for the positions you are targeting, you can build a comprehensive Job Skills Portfolio. Now you will be able to compare the skills you have with the ones employers are looking for. Following are the simple steps to creating your portfolio.

What is a Job Skills Portfolio? It is an instrument that gives employers with whom you are interviewing a comprehensive picture of you—your experience, education, skills, and evidence of your work background. Your question about now is probably, *"But I already have those items in my resume and cover letter."* However, a Job Skills Portfolio is more than a resume and cover letter because it allows you to include items that wouldn't be acceptable in your resume or cover letter. Whereas in the past it was generally used more by those in creative fields such graphic arts, education, entertainment, and so on, it is now a practice that job seekers use in many different occupations.

To begin, you need to determine how you're going to organize your portfolio. As with any presentation, draw up a table of contents to give you an outline of what you are going to include. This table will be governed by what attributes you have to offer employers. They should be the skills and abilities that will encourage them to offer you the job. Remember to *match* yours with those you know companies are looking for.

TELEPHONE LOG

Date _____   Telephone Number _____

Name of Company _____

Address of Company _____

Name of Contact Person _____   E-mail _____

Information Interview _____   Position(s) Open _____

No Openings _____   Future Contact Date _____

Comments _____

Date _____   Telephone Number _____

Name of Company _____

Address of Company _____

Name of Contact Person _____   E-mail _____

Information Interview _____   Position(s) Open _____

No Openings _____   Future Contact Date _____

Comments _____

Date _____   Telephone Number _____

Name of Company _____

Address of Company _____

Name of Contact Person _____   E-mail _____

Information Interview _____   Position(s) Open _____

No Openings _____   Future Contact Date _____

Comments _____

INFORMATIONAL INTERVIEW RECORD

Date of Interview

Name of Company

Address

Name and title of person being interviewed

Phone Number   E-mail

Time spent interviewing

What information did you gain from the interview?

Was the interview useful to you?   Did you enjoy it?

Comments

INFORMATIONAL INTERVIEW RECORD

Date of Interview

Name of Company

Address

Name and title of person being interviewed

Phone Number   E-mail

Time spent interviewing

What information did you gain from the interview?

Was the interview useful to you?   Did you enjoy it?

Comments

Here are some suggestions for possible items you might wish to include in your portfolio, always keeping in mind your best points that demonstrate who you are and what you can provide to the company to which you will be interviewing. Much of this information you can gather from your strength inventory and skills /abilities assessment you completed in Chapter 1. Although photos are rarely included in resumes, they can be added to your portfolio. But only if they show you in a favorable light, possibly at work or in a formal presentation, should you use them. *Caution: get a second opinion to be certain the photos are evidence of your best capabilities.*

1. *Education and Relevant Training* All transcipts, certificates of training, degrees, and licenses. All conferences and/or workshops, including the program material that was covered.
2. *Past Work Experience* Job descriptions with itemized job duties, lists of transferable and functional skills, samples of your work, resumes— scannable and traditional paper copies, favorable employer evaluations and reviews. You can include CDs if you have them.
3. *Achievements* Awards, letters of recommendation and commendation, merit documents, improvements in the workplace, and innovative, original creations.
4. *Work-Related Marketable Skills* Problem solving, leadership, investigation, and prioritizing.
5. *Volunteer Programs, Community Service Projects.* Any community service program such as tutoring, mentoring, youth group aid or instructor, where you volunteered your time and/or expertise.
6. *Publications, Reports, Research* This can be an opportunity to demonstrate many abilities, especially written communications skills. It can include any manuscript, essay, or publication in local or national bulletins, news articles, books, and so on.

Once you have written and gathered all of the samples, information, photos, and lists you want to include, you are ready to put your portfolio together in a professional manner. Enclose it in a quality binder with a title page, a table of contents, and possibly some section dividers for easy access. Keep the documents clean, neat, and fresh. The title page is placed at the beginning, and immediately after that, you need to include your goals statement (where you see yourself in three to five years). Some career counselors suggest that in the beginning section, you add a statement of your work ethics, interests, and management principles. I agree this is important but only if you are clear on how to compose and produce a well-written statement.

Finally, before you reproduce copies of your portfolio, have someone with impeccable written communications skills proofread it for you. It's even advisable to have more than one person proofread your documents to guarantee there are no errors in them. Believe me, if there is one, the interviewer will find it; that is another one of Murphy's laws.

As I explained previously, the first assignment in organizing your job search is to list companies you would like to work for, get information on those companies, and acquire job title descriptions. Now you are ready for the second part of that assignment, which is to find the job openings. Some statistics that will influence your search for job openings are as follows. *U.S. News & World Report*, in an article "Where the Jobs for Grads Are" in MSN Money, lists the most promising

LIBRARY SEARCH REPORTS

Source Information (title of publication, website URL, etc.)

_____

Name of Company _____

Address _____

Phone Number(s) _____

Contact Person _____

Summary of important and useful information _____

_____

_____

_____

_____

_____

_____

_____

Source Information (title of publication, website URL, etc.)

_____

Name of Company _____

Address _____

Phone Number(s) _____

Contact Person _____

Summary of important and useful information _____

_____

_____

_____

_____

_____

_____

_____

LIBRARY SEARCH REPORTS

Source Information (title of publication, website URL, etc.)

_____

Name of Company _____

Address _____

Phone Number(s) _____

Contact Person _____

Summary of important and useful information _____

_____

_____

_____

_____

_____

_____

_____

Source Information (title of publication, website URL, etc.)

_____

Name of Company _____

Address _____

Phone Number(s) _____

Contact Person _____

Summary of important and useful information _____

_____

_____

_____

_____

_____

_____

_____

employment categories as "software development, financial services, human resources, and administration." Warren Kistner, director of the career center at Illinois Wesleyan University, in the same article says, "There are definite differences in terms of supply and demand by state, so students must be aware of the market."[2]

Therefore, as you look for the job you desire, keep these things in mind.

Where Are the Jobs?

There are many ways to find job openings. Approaches to finding job leads can vary with some industries, but for 98 percent of the positions available, you can employ any or all of the methods listed here. When you are looking for work, use all available resources for a successful job search. The more you use, the sooner you'll find the job you want. Most job searchers mass-market themselves by indiscriminately mailing hundreds of resumes, believing this method will get interviews and, ultimately, a job. Not true! This is the most *inactive* way to job search; it could take you months or even a year to find a job this way, especially if the job market is down. The only effective way is to focus your search *actively* using the following strategies.

Newspapers and Trade Publications

The classified section of the newspaper is, as you probably already know, a good place to begin your quest. However, you need to know how to get the most mileage from this source. There is nothing wrong with using the classifieds, but you should know that only a very small percentage of the available jobs at any given time are ever advertised, and the competition for advertised jobs is extremely high. The average ad, depending on the field and the job market, of course, nets anywhere from 75 to 300+ resumes. Consequently, your chances of getting an interview, much less getting a job offer, from a classified ad could be very slim. If you are going to use the classifieds, use the techniques described here to maximize your efforts.

Check prior newspaper ads.   When you begin your job search, go to the library or to someone you know who saves newspapers and collect all of the Sunday and Wednesday issues for the past 10 to 12 weeks. Why? Well, think about it. What is the probationary period for most jobs? That's right, 60 to 90 days. During this period, the employer is considering whether or not to keep the person they've hired. If the employer is not going to retain the employee, the chances are that he or she is dreading the prospect of advertising, interviewing, and selecting another employee. Also, many times companies are unable to find someone to fill the job and continue to look long after the ad runs. For either reason, if you are qualified, the company will be delighted to hear from you.

Expand your search.   When you are deciding which ads to respond to, consider ads for positions that are a little above or below what you are actually seeking. Employers are often willing to talk to you about upgrading or downgrading a job if they see that you could be a contributor to their company. Look for ads for related positions. Notice those businesses advertising for sales or accounting personnel. If they are advertising for these positions, this could indicate that they may be planning to increase their business by adding more services or products. They might need people with your skills. Always check the ads for part-time and temp positions because many are tryouts for full-time positions. Employers many times hire persons as temporary to examine how they can or cannot handle the job before giving permanent status and benefits. Many times blind ads are placed for legitimate jobs and employers use them to avoid being deluged with nuisance calls of people phoning to beg for interviews, so go ahead and check them out, but not if you think that your employer might have placed it.

Read the business section of the paper. This is where you will find out about new companies coming to your area, branch offices opening up, expansions in already existing firms, and the names of people being promoted to positions of management. If you're really serious about making some good contacts, send a letter of congratulations on the promotion and include a resume (a nice gesture that just might get you an interview).

Read the trade journals for your industry. You will find articles and advertisements that will give you information on companies to contact. Many of these journals also have classified ad sections that list job opportunities. Even if the ads are not for the kind of position you are looking for, again, they could indicate growth and that openings may be coming soon in other areas. Some trade journals list meetings and conventions that could be useful in your job search. If you're looking for positions with specific firms, you might be able to attend these functions and make contacts with key personnel.

Associations

The *Encyclopedia of Associations* gives the names and addresses of trade associations that are affiliated with all industries. These associations are always looking for new members and are usually happy to speak with job hunters like you. Many times they will invite you to one of their monthly or quarterly meetings, where they sometimes have workshops or dinners. It is a wonderful and fun way to obtain many contacts with local companies in your industry. And if you do become a member, it is a definite plus to be able to add it to your resume.

State and City Job Service Centers

These are employment agencies operated by the government and are open to the general public. They have free daily listings of jobs within your state and city. The listings are usually for lower-level, minimum-wage jobs, but sometimes these entry-level openings are with companies that offer advancement.

Career Fairs

Matt Berndt, director of career services for the College of Communication at the University of Texas, said, "Employers are coming to job and internship fairs in record numbers."[3] Attending career fairs can allow you to talk with many employers in one day. Fairs are usually held in large hotels or convention centers and feature many of the larger companies in your area, along with others from all over the country. Dress as if you are going to an interview, and take several copies of your resume with you. The companies usually do not hire at career fairs, but they do take resumes and applications. The majority of them will be looking for persons with at least a bachelor's degree; however, don't let this intimidate you if you don't have one. Speak with them anyway, and sell what you do have! Not all organizations are locked in to these requirements; most take an honest look at anyone who is positive and enthusiastic. Be prepared for wall-to-wall people, and get a good night's sleep before you go. In times of high unemployment and particularly in the spring when hundreds of college graduates are looking for jobs, these fairs can be swamped with job applicants.

Chambers of Commerce

Most companies register with the local Chamber of Commerce, and new businesses use this membership for advertising and promoting themselves in their communities. Be sure to ask if there is a charge for the chamber's handout materials; some charge a fee. If you are relocating to another state or city, the Chamber of Commerce is one of the first places you should visit to receive a wealth of information about all of the activities and companies in their cities. I did this when I relocated from Denver to Southern California and had three offers for jobs and invitations to societies within a couple of weeks. Trust me, it does work!

Career Resources and College Placement Centers

If you are a graduate of any college, the career resource or placement center is the first place you should go. Nearly all technical, business, and community colleges provide placement assistance for their graduates. Universities are now realizing that they must offer more services for their graduates and are expanding their career resource centers to include their alumni. Recruiters from companies all over the United States visit colleges regularly to interview potential employees.

Remember that your placement or employment assistance office will provide you with job leads; however, it is still your responsibility to duplicate those efforts and conduct your own intensive search. If you want a job soon after, or even before, you graduate, the possibility of this is greater if *both* of you are seeking.

College placement centers are excellent sources for information on employers, even if you are not a graduate, because they have daily contact with employers and know what kinds of applicants companies look for. They also know the current salary ranges offered by a lot of the companies.

Bulletin Boards

Many public places have bulletin boards where companies post job listings. Check the boards at state and city government offices, libraries, courthouses, supermarkets, and recreational centers. These can be viable sources for job leads.

Temporary Service Agencies

Temporary agencies are a reliable source for job openings. Temporary agencies match up employees with employers who need short-term help in just about every field. As mentioned earlier, companies appreciate the freedom to add an employee for a short time without the commitment of permanency or the cost of benefits. Temp agencies contract you out to these companies, and they pay your salary, which is usually lower than the going rate. This can be a good way to get your foot in the door of well-established firms who might not hire you directly. In addition, statistics show that the length of time that temporary employees stay with an agency varies from three to five weeks because many times they are hired by the client firm. If you are changing careers and have little or no experience in the field you are entering, temporary positions are an excellent way to get that experience.

Job Placement Firms

Be very cautious about using job placement firms. A scam alert from the *AARP Bulletin* warns job seekers about placement firms that ask for money up front and guarantee you a job in your field but never deliver. "The Council of Better Business Bureaus logged more than 1,000 complaints last year involving job placement services. If you are going to use a job placement firm, you should always ask how long they have been in business and what their success rate has been for placing clients in jobs."[4] Believe me, *no one* can guarantee you a job. For more information on how to protect yourself from unscrupulous job placement firms, visit the AARP website, www.aarp.org/bulletin/scamalert.

Direct Contact: Visits or Calls to Potential Employers

You've probably heard of the so-called hidden job market and wondered where it was and how to find it. Well, there's no mysterious secret; it exists all the time, and the way you find it is simply to contact companies directly. Openings are created every day in all organizations by terminations, retirements, and deaths, as well as by relocations, resignations, and promotions. When you call or visit employers directly, you will discover this hidden market. Telephoning and visiting the company are two of the most effective ways to find job openings, and more jobs are acquired in this way than through more traditional methods. Because you make the contact before employers have advertised or announced the opening, you have the opportunity to present your qualifications ahead of everyone else. The advantage of using the telephone is that you can reach more companies in a shorter time. If you go in person, however, you may be offered an interview on the spot, so be prepared!

Using the U.S. Postal Service

Mailing resumes and cover letters may be something that just about all job seekers do, but it is the least productive. Your return on mailing resumes, if you are lucky, is probably about 1 percent. It is so easy for employers to send you a rejection letter in the mail or, worse, to ignore your resume completely. Because so many people approach job searching in this way, the competition is staggering. If you are going to mail resumes, be selective and follow the guidelines given in Chapter 2 (with respect to who gets the resume). Remember that in today's market, your documents are very likely to be scanned, so use a 10 by 13-inch envelope. The larger envelope gives you an advantage over other applicants who don't know this. You want your letter and resume to arrive flat and unfolded, scanner ready. Folded, the creases in your resume may damage your document's text, and the scanner may not be able to read it. If you haven't received a response from the company in a week (for small companies) or three weeks (for larger companies), send a second resume and call if you have the number.

Networking

You've probably heard the saying, "It's not what you know, but who you know." Well, when it comes to job searching, this could be true, which could be a source of frustration for some job seekers. They may feel that people who benefit from family or monetary connections are dishonest or unethical. Using your connections to find openings and to get an opportunity to interview is very acceptable.

Most of the best jobs are never advertised. Organizations themselves do their own networking when they need new employees. They consult with their current employees, vendors, customers, and so on. Many of the firms I have worked with over the years have told me that 30 to 40 percent of their openings are filled by a referral from one of the sources just listed. One of the reasons that job seekers miss valuable connections to job openings is that they fail to network. Contacts are paramount in a job search; the bigger your list of qualified prospects, the faster you will get interviews and ultimately the job. *Networking* is one of the most effective and productive ways of getting leads and job offers and also gets you access to people who might not respond to a direct approach letter. At least 60 percent—some even report higher statistics—of all jobs are found by networking. Develop contacts: friends, family, neighbors, college alumni, and so on. This is also a source for the hidden job market. **Networking** is telling everyone you know that you are looking for a job and what kind of positions you seek.

Making an assumption that your family and friends know what kind of job you are seeking could be a grave error; they probably don't. Be sure that you tell them what you're looking for in a job. When I ask the people in my job search workshops and classes how many of their families could describe the kind of job they are looking for, very rarely do any hands go up.

Talk with everyone you meet about your job goal, even at social gatherings. At any gathering, people will be talking in groups. Casually join a group and take a moment to tune in to the conversation. Don't monopolize the conversation; listen. You can learn a lot by listening. Ask people where they work and if they know of any openings. You are probably doing this right now without even being aware of it. Think about it: How many people have you associated with in the past month? Did you talk about your job search? I'll bet you did. Now is not the time to be shy, proud, or zealous about your privacy; you have to open your mouth and ask. If you are very shy and just can't bring yourself to speak up, volunteer to work at the registration table where you can greet people as they come in or get some inexpensive "Situation Wanted" cards printed to give to people. You can buy them like business cards or make your own, very inexpensively, with one of the many low-cost software packages on the market. There are also networking groups you can join such as the Five O'Clock Club, a premier outplacement career coaching organization with a monthly fee of $40 (no, it isn't a supper club with belly dancers). The number to call is 800-538-6645. There is also the 40-Plus Club (202-387-1582) with an initiation fee of $600 and monthly costs of $30.

As well as networking the usual traditional way, job seekers now are using the Internet for just about everything, including finding job leads. Just go to Google and key in something like "networking" or "job leads," and you will discover e-mail listservs, mail-based discussion forums such as APA (American Psychological Association), and message boards. Vault's message boards focuses on careers and education. There's the Wetfeet.com industry and company boards that can give you information on career fields and employers. One website that focuses on online *job search and career networking* provides a link to Kelly Career Network. This link gives choices of states and job titles and can lead you to actual job openings where you can apply online.

To begin your networking process, complete the worksheet "Networking Prospects" with as many names as you can. Who's number one on your prospective employer list? How many people know you, trust you, and want you to do well in your career? You should probably come up with at least 200 names. Plan to contact at least 10 people every day.

NETWORKING PROSPECTS

List the names of all the people, businesses, groups, etc. that could be sources for leads or referrals.

Family
_____
_____

Friends
_____
_____

Neighbors
_____
_____

Service suppliers (grocers, service stations, etc.)
_____
_____

Former employers, coworkers
_____
_____

Schools, colleges, churches
_____
_____

Clubs, associations, memberships
_____
_____

People and companies from the business cards you collected
_____
_____
_____

Searching for Jobs on the Internet

The previous discussion focused on the many sources for finding job openings with some suggestions and websites for using the Internet for job leads. The Internet *is* a valuable source because it offers enough job bank sites to fill a book. Although it hasn't totally replaced conventional methods of job searching, the Internet has become a vital tool for searching hundreds of job databases, job listings, and company websites around the globe. If you plan to post your resume, you must prepare one that can be read by software or computer systems. *Caution:* Before posting your resume on the Internet, if you are currently employed, be sure the site guarantees confidentiality, and *don't mail it from your employer's address.* Companies sometimes search the Net on their own names. (See Chapter 2 for instructions for preparing an electronic resume.)

Corporate Internet Sites

Many companies and public organizations have established their own websites and include vacancy announcements online. They also now put their Web addresses in their newspaper ads. The vacancies listed on a company's site contain more information than the ones published in newspaper ads, often giving an e-mail address, a fax number, and a postal address. If you don't have a definite company that you want to work for but want to investigate some corporate sites, go to Yahoo! (www.yahoo.com), then click on the link "Hot Jobs—Thousands of jobs. Find the right one." For classified ads from major U.S. newspapers, go to www.careerpath.com.

Internet Job Banks

The Internet offers hundreds of job banks with information about job openings, companies, and job search services. Job banks often change their names and URLs, and some will close as new ones appear. The following URLs were current as of this writing.

> www.jobbankinfo.org
> Canada's Job Bank: www.jobbank.gc.ca
> CareerPath: www.careerpath.com
> CareerBuilder (searches by location): www.careerbuilder.com
> Hotjobs.com: www.hotjobs.com
> Monster.com: www.monster.com
> Joboptions: www.joboptions.com

Other notable job banks include the following:

> www.careerfile.com
> www.jobs.com (global and local)
> www.careermart.com; link: www.apha.org/about/careers—gives information on Public Health careers
> www2.jobtrak.com—specific college & university career centers
> www.headhunter.net—refines by location with a link "DexKnows.com"
> www.taonline.com—transition assistance for moving from military to civilian life

SEARCHING THE INTERNET

To test your competence in searching the Internet, select a job bank or a corporate site and go online to find openings for the job you desire. If you have difficulty finding a site or would prefer a fast search, try using a search engine. Search engines scan the Web for keywords you specify. A few popular search engines are at www.altavista.com, www.hotbot.com, and www.metacrawler.com. For best results, use quotation marks for phrases "you want to appear exactly as typed," be specific, and enter more than one keyword to narrow your search.

JobCircle.com—regional job board for job seekers in Pennsylvania, New York, New Jersey, Delaware, Maryland, and Washington, D.C.

Focus your online search as narrowly as possible, whether it is for a particular industry or geographic location. Pick the right sites, those directly related to the field you have chosen. Be certain to keep track of who you've e-mailed and where you have posted so you can follow up. If you don't know where to begin, refer to the suggestions in the nearby box.

Planning   "Fail to Plan, Plan to Fail"

Careful planning and good time management are of the utmost importance when you begin your job search. Procrastinating and delaying are usually the result of poor organization, and a lack of organization is a direct result of a failure to plan. So as you can see, one leads to the other, which leads you to *nowhere*. Because almost everyone is prone to procrastination, you need a workable plan in order not to fall victim to this trap when you are job searching. In a job search, procrastination means missing appointments, interviews, and, ultimately, a job.

Your job search plan should include some realistic objectives for each day of your search, a deadline for each weekly goal, and checkpoints to monitor your activity and your progress. Setting goals and listing some definite actions to acquire those goals will keep you motivated and help you to deal with rejection in a positive way. Go back to your goals worksheet and review the steps you listed there. You will be better prepared for your interviews and feel a lot less anxiety and frustration.

View your job search as a full-time job because that's exactly what it is. Of course, you do need to schedule some time for relaxation, but don't get offtrack by taking time out to clean the closets, paint the downstairs bedroom, or anything else that can wait until after you land that job. It only makes it more difficult to get started again if you lose your momentum. Keep with your plan, and remember that persistence always pays off!

These are the particulars of a well-organized job search:

- Make your job search a 40-hour week.
- Once you begin your search, keep going until you have your job.
- Always plan your week in advance.
- Always begin your day early.

- Make calls and visits to employers every day.
- Follow up on leads, requests for resumes, and so on, immediately.
- If you are currently employed, make calls or visits on your lunch hour. You can also take some personal leave days to interview. Employers may be willing to meet with you after hours, even on Saturday if they are interested in you.

The Daily Performance Planner and the Performance Record sheets on the following pages will help you get started and keep going. Begin by setting up your daily performance plan for each day of the week. At the end of the week, summarize your progress and fill in your plan for the next week. Analyze what you are doing and the results you are getting as you go along so you can assess your progress realistically. If you are not getting interviews, or if you are interviewing but not getting offers, examine what you're doing or not doing. Spend some time to figure out a new game plan and find solutions to these problems. Maybe you need to take a serious look at your resume or call the employers who have interviewed you and ask for frank, constructive feedback. Have you been procrastinating? Are you selling yourself? An honest evaluation of your activity is always helpful to get you back on track. Search for other job seekers, possibly classmates you graduated with. Also, check with the Career Development office of your college to see if it has meetings for graduates who are still looking for work. A lot can be said for getting together with others who are in the same situation that you are for sharing information, leads, and tips on what works or doesn't work.

DAILY PERFORMANCE PLANNER

Date: _____

Job Search Activities:

NAME/ADDRESS OF CONTACT	VISIT, CALL, MAILING	RESULT
1. _____	_____	_____
_____	_____	_____
2. _____	_____	_____
_____	_____	_____
3. _____	_____	_____
_____	_____	_____
4. _____	_____	_____
_____	_____	_____
5. _____	_____	_____
_____	_____	_____
6. _____	_____	_____
_____	_____	_____
7. _____	_____	_____
_____	_____	_____
8. _____	_____	_____
_____	_____	_____
9. _____	_____	_____
_____	_____	_____
10. _____	_____	_____
_____	_____	_____

PERFORMANCE RECORD AND SUMMARY

Week of

Total contacts made

Number of interviews

Job leads acquired

Follow-up needed

NOTES

1. Paul J. Lim, "Money Watch," *U.S. News & World Report,* April 30, 2007, 67. Copyright U.S. News & World Report, L.P. Reprinted with permission.

2. "Where the Jobs for Grads Are," *U.S. News & World Report*, e-mail survey by the National Association of Colleges and Employers, May 21, 2007. Copyright U.S. News & World Report, L.P. Reprinted with permission.

3. Ibid.

4. "Bum Job Leads," *AARP Bulletin*, June 2004, 22.

Interviewing Made *Almost* Easy

Of all the phases of job searching, from writing your resume to the time you say "yes" to a job offer, the one most traumatizing to job seekers is the interview. No wonder: The interview is the most critical part of the job search. *The interview is where you are hired or not hired.* It's the zero hour, and you must be prepared to be scrutinized. During the interview, you are the "bug under the glass," to put it bluntly.

4

C H A P T E R

What can you do to minimize the fears, the anxiety, the sweaty palms? How can you get through the interviewing process with your self-confidence intact and get the job you want? That's what this chapter is about: helping you take the fear out of interviewing and showing you that you *can* have the job you desire. No matter what your age is or what field you're in, you can use certain strategies and techniques that will help you handle this phase of the job search with more confidence and less stress. Knowing how companies conduct interviews, what their expectations are of you as a prospective employee, what subjective assumptions are made in 75 to 80 percent of all interviews, and how to evaluate your performance are just a few of the tools that can make interviewing *almost* easy.

How *Not* to Interview

onsider some of these most common mistakes that will keep you from being hired:

- Not conducting the necessary research on the company and the industry.
- Not practicing (role playing) for interviews.
- Not knowing the job requirements.
- Improper dress or sloppy appearance.
- Giving inappropriate or untruthful answers to interview questions.
- Not having questions to ask the interviewer other than "What are the salary and benefits?"
- Poor communication skills and body language that "give you away."
- Criticizing former employers or supervisors.
- Not selling yourself, being too passive, lacking enthusiasm.
- Not knowing salary ranges and your worth.
- Lack of career direction and goals.
- Not knowing how to close the interview.
- Overemphasizing money.
- Being late to the interview.
- Sharing a marked dislike for schoolwork.
- Failing to follow up after the interview

Trying to impress an interviewer, job seekers have done some very strange things in interviews. Over the many years I have dealt with employers and helped people find jobs, I've been informed of some very unusual interview conduct. One I remember so well was when an employer called and said she didn't know whether to hire this student I had sent. When I asked her what the problem was, she said, "Well, when my husband took him for a tour of our company, his wife started begging and pleading for us to hire him." The employer said that the wife told her, "If you don't hire him, I'm afraid my husband will commit suicide." Did they hire the student? What do you think?

In this chapter you will learn how to avoid the common pitfalls. Some of those pitfalls are not preparing properly for the interview, not selling yourself, and not dressing professionally. You will learn how employers conduct interviews and what they are really looking for, what the necessary preparation is, and how to sell yourself. Chapter 5 concludes the discussion of the interview process and shows you where to find information on salary ranges, how to negotiate for a reasonable and equitable salary, what to do between interviews, and how to deal with rejection. Interviewing is not as difficult as most people think. Yes, it does make you feel very vulnerable. After all, the interviewer could say, "Sorry, you don't measure up; you're not what we're looking for." And that hurts! It is not an attack on your self-worth, and you can save yourself a lot of agony if you prepare for your interviews properly and know how to present yourself to a prospective employer confidently and professionally. You will have a much greater chance of getting the job of your choice and dealing with rejections effectively.

I can promise you this: If you do your homework, follow the suggestions in this chapter, and remember to believe in yourself, interviewing will be less fearful than it has ever been. Who knows? You might even consider it an exciting challenge.

Successful Interview Preparation

Preparation, the first step to successful interviewing, is the most neglected. People searching for work usually do not have the vaguest idea how to prepare for an interview correctly. And not being prepared creates about 75 percent of your fear. You simply cannot expect to make a favorable impression on the employer who is interviewing you if you do not prepare yourself beforehand. First, you must know something about the company to which you are applying. If you go into the interview with no idea what this company does, you are asking for rejection. It is an insult to them that you didn't care enough to find out what they're all about, and the last thing you want to do is to ask them about their company in the interview. In the beginning of this chapter, I listed some ways on how *not* to interview. One of those is "not selling yourself," a number-one reason employers give for not hiring an applicant. Therefore, a most important element in your interview preparation is knowing how to sell yourself to the prospective employer. This can be done successfully by constructing some benefit statements.

Benefits You Can Sell to the Employer

When you are writing your resume and being interviewed, it is not enough to make *generalized* statements to an employer. Making a **generalization** (a statement that implies rather than giving facts, specifics, and information) to a prospective employer is risky unless you back it up with evidence. To convince an employer of your worth, you must give specifics. How do you prove to an employer that you are dependable, flexible, able to cope with technological change, and so on? An effective way of presenting yourself is to prepare some carefully constructed, well-thought-out statements of your abilities with examples that illustrate them. These are called **benefit statements.**

A good benefit statement has three parts: It begins with a statement of your skill, ability, or knowledge. It then gives examples of when and where you demonstrated or learned it, in other words, *proof* that you actually have it. The key selling factor of a benefit statement is the third part: informing the employer how and why it will benefit him or her. To do this, you must put yourself in the place of the employer. If you were the employer and this were your company, what would help you to be profitable and successful?

The more explicit you can be, the better. Give facts, figures, *quantitative evidence* of your knowledge or experience in the stated area. Don't simply restate the ability that you gave in part one. When you tell employers how your ability will benefit them, remember that the bottom line for all companies is saving time and making money. How could your skill of problem solving, for instance, save them time and money? Try to relate the skill directly to their specialized needs.

To write effective benefit statements that will sell you to an employer, you should have done some informational interviews and researched positions such as those listed in the *DOT (Dictionary of Occupational Titles)* and the *OOH (Occupational Outlook Handbook)* discussed in Chapter 3. This research will have given you a good idea of the skills and abilities required for the position(s) you are seeking.

Here are some examples of benefit statements. Study them so that you can skillfully prepare some of your best selling points and construct three to five benefit statements for presenting to an employer.

Sample Benefit Statements

Skill: I am a detail-oriented person.

Proof: When I was working for United Aviation and in the Marine Corps, I followed step-by-step procedures, schematics, drawings, and prints. I troubleshot and pinpointed problems on systems using schematics. I fabricated parts to the customer's drawings.

Benefit to an employer: I will follow instructions to the detail, thereby saving time by doing things correctly the first time. This is a benefit to any employer because not following instructions and having to do things over is costly in terms of profit and time.

Skill: I am a dependable person.

Proof: While in the military for four years, I never missed a day. I now work full time and attend school full time and still always complete my work duties, assignments, and tasks on time.

Benefit to an employer: He or she can always count on me to be there, to complete the tasks given to me, on time. All in all, I will get the job done and done right.

Skill: I am flexible and adaptable to unscheduled priorities.

Proof: Throughout my career, last-minute things have always come up. For a vehicle that goes down that has high priority and needs to be fixed immediately or a late order that needs to be filled quickly, I am able to adapt quickly and get the job done.

Benefit to an employer: I am able to adapt to different and unplanned schedules, work habits, and policies. I understand that sometimes last-minute things need to be completed. Therefore, I am willing to stay late and work extra hours to get them done.

Skill: I have excellent time-management skills.

Proof: While attending college to obtain my degree and working 50 hours a week for Commnet Cellular as a senior systems engineer, I still carried a 4.0 GPA in school.

Benefit to an employer: This ability will allow me to complete more projects in a timely manner, thereby offering you a more productive workforce and an increase in profits by eliminating your need to pay overtime.

Skill: I am a stable and dependable person.

Proof: I have been in the workforce for 15 years and have had only two employers. I was in the U.S. Air Force for eight years and have worked for Commnet Cellular for seven years.

Benefit to an employer: This benefits your company because you will not have to spend time and money training me only to worry about my leaving your company. You would not have to hire a replacement and spend money and time in retraining.

Skill: Leadership is one of my strongest qualities.

Proof: One of my responsibilities at Commnet Cellular was to implement digital technology as an overlay to our analog system. This required coordinating and managing multiple departments to ensure that everything was done. The project was completed one and a half months ahead of schedule.

Benefit to an employer: Leadership is always needed in all progressive companies. Employers want to be sure that when they delegate responsibility for a project to someone, that person will be able to coordinate all departments, stimulate cooperative teamwork, and complete the project on time. I can do this.

Skill: I am a very creative and original thinker.

Proof: I have the ability to picture in my mind the design I am going to make. My house is full of all the designs I created while in school. This is why I chose to become a draftsperson. My college instructors chose me to mentor and assist other students with their drawings.

Benefit to an employer: Profits are gained from new and repeat customers. I will be able to come up with fresh, new ideas that will be what the customer wants. This will attract new customers and keep them coming back.

Skill: One of my greatest strengths is excellent communication skills. I can express myself clearly, both orally and in writing.

Proof: At Quality Insurance, where I worked for five years, I was responsible for dealing directly with the customers who were filing claims. I was able to assist them effectively, over the phone and in person, by listening carefully and then transcribing the information correctly for the claims adjustors. This saved time and kept the customers happy because their claims were identified and handled quickly.

Benefit to an employer: I believe you would find this skill very useful in your business because listening to customers and identifying what they need is critical to good business and repeat business.

BENEFIT STATEMENTS

Go back through the previous worksheets that you've completed and choose your major skills and abilities. Write at least five, preferably more, benefit statements of your own. The more you have, the better equipped you'll be to persuade an employer to interview you or to offer you the job.

Skill #1

_____

_____

Proof

_____

_____

_____

Benefit to the employer

_____

_____

_____

Skill #2

_____

_____

Proof

_____

_____

_____

Benefit to the employer

_____

_____

_____

Skill #3

_____

_____

Proof

_____

_____

_____

Benefit to the employer

_____

_____

_____

Use a blank sheet of paper for more benefit statements.

The Bottom Line

Knowing yourself and what you have to offer, plus having a definite direction and showing you have it are the keys to marketing yourself successfully to a prospective employer. A salesperson would never think of trying to sell a product to a customer without knowing everything there is to know about that product—what it can and cannot do, what its strong and weak points are—and having answers for any questions the customer might raise about that product. It is no different when you are job searching; you are both the product *and* the salesperson.

If you have completed the exercises on the preceding pages, you are now ready to summarize your assets and create a personal profile, your "marketing appraisal." Here is an example of what it might look like:

I have the personal characteristics of honesty, loyalty, reliability, integrity, and sincerity needed for successful and productive job performance in my industry. I am cost-conscious in terms of materials, time, and personnel and am flexible and adaptable in dealing effectively with change in the workplace.

I have a proven record in troubleshooting and problem solving and have been consistently rated a top performer in my job appraisals. I have a positive attitude that is demonstrated by my ability to be a cooperative team player and to work successfully with my coworkers and supervisors.

I am open-minded, perceptive, and diplomatic in my interactions with customers and business clients. I produce accurate and timely work and am ready to be a productive employee for your organization.

After you've completed your benefit statements and have written your marketing appraisal, you are now ready to research the companies where you have found openings and/or those with which you have interviews scheduled.

What Does the Company Do?

It's actually quite easy to research companies. Now is the time to put your library and Internet techniques to use. Using the guidelines in Chapter 3, learn as much as

MY MARKETING APPRAISAL

(What I Can Offer an Employer)

_____

_____

_____

_____

_____

_____

_____

_____

_____

_____

you can about the company to which you are applying. Interviewers try to determine not only your interest in obtaining the job, but also why you wish to work for them as opposed to other companies. Two questions they may ask are "What do you know about our company?" and "What contribution can you make to our organization?" To answer these questions knowledgeably, you must have done your research. The more information you have on the company, the better qualified you will be to answer their questions about your ability to contribute to their growth and prosperity—which is, by the way, the most important thing to them. Use these lists of library and Internet sources to assist you in your search for information on companies; the latter were taken from the *Cyberspace Job Search Kit*.

LIBRARY RESEARCH SOURCES (can be researched on the Web also)

- *New York Times Index.* Twice monthly index of newspaper articles in the *New York Times*, according to subject matter, dates, etc. You can sign up to receive free daily briefing of an e-newsletter.

- *Applied Science & Technology Index.* Index of articles from magazines devoted to aeronautics, automation, chemistry, construction, metallurgy, transportation, and other related subjects. Covers subjects alphabetically from acoustics to waste management and other industrial and mechanical arts.

- *Facts on File.* Weekly 8- to 10-page news digest that gives unbiased coverage of significant news events of each day, indexed for easy location.

- *Information Please Almanac.* In addition to statistical information, it features brief articles summarizing developments in various fields during the previous year.

- *World Almanac.* One-volume yearly publication that presents statistics on business, education, industries, governments, population, sports, foreign countries, etc.

- *Business Periodicals Index.* Indexes more than 100 magazines in accounting, advertising, banking, business, insurance, labor, and other related fields and covers acquisitions and mergers.

Libraries also provide access to CD-ROMs such as InfoTrac and ProQuest, which are collections of magazine articles, and microfiche copies of newspapers and journal articles.

INTERNET SITES FOR EMPLOYER INFORMATION[1]

- *EDGAR.* The Electronic Data Gathering, Analysis, and Retrieval system. Contains the publicly available filings submitted to the Securities and Exchange Commission (SEC). At this site, you can find a public company's annual report, or 10-K, which describes the company's overall direction and includes financial data, information on research projects in development, and other plans. www.sec.gov/edgar.shtml

- *Hoover's Online.* Contains "company capsules" on every U.S. company traded on a major stock exchange, as well as some 2,000 private companies, that offer information on recent reports, brief financial data, and links to each company's website. www.hoovers.com

- *Forbes 500 Largest Private Companies.* Includes a brief company description, number of employees, sales rank, and a link to the company's website, www .forbes.com/private500. They issue a free *Forbes* magazine at www.forbes.com.

- *Companies Online.* A joint project of Lycos and Dun & Bradstreet that includes private companies. www.companiesonline.com
- *Fortune. Fortune* magazine's 100 Best Companies to Work for in America. www.fortune.com/fortune/bestcompanies/index.html gives the 2008 full list.
- *Fortune.* The magazine's ranking of the most admired companies. www.fortune.com/fortune/mostadmired/index.html
- *Women's Wire. Women's Wire's* list of the best companies in the United States for women, based on salary, benefits, and opportunities for advancement. www.womenswire.com (bottom of page, key in city, state, ZIP for localized search)
- *Working Woman.* Contains the magazine's list of the top 500 women-owned companies. www.workingwomanmag.com
- *The Hispanic Business 500 directory.* www.hispanicbusiness.com/research/companies/default.asp supplies information on diversity issues.

Where Is the Company Located?

Another vital step in preparing for a successful interview is to make certain you know exactly where the company is located and how to get there. Don't make the grave error of thinking you know approximately where it is and then end up walking in late for the interview because you didn't know for sure. When you schedule the interview, ask for directions. If you forget to ask, call and find out. Ask about parking: Is there a special lot or space for visitors? Is it controlled by security? Find out if there is more than one building, and if so, which one you are to go to. Next, if at all possible, take a trial run to the business so that you are prepared for any detours, street repairs, and so on. By doing this, you will also know how long it takes to get there. Take into account the hour of the day when you will be interviewing. Is it during the rush hour? If so, be sure to allow sufficient extra time, depending on the distance.

What *Is* Professional Dress?

The question of dress usually brings up a lot of discussion and different ideas about what is or is not professional. Unfortunately, there is no one simple way to describe, for everyone, what it is. One thing you can be sure of: Your overall appearance can help or hinder a hiring decision. A few years ago, the concept of what is professional dress in the workplace underwent a dramatic change. In many companies, suits and ties were replaced with the "Dockers look," and "casual Friday" became a common trend. It appears that the concept of professional dress changes with the values of society as it has now in the twenty-first century. I am now hearing from some employers that the casual Friday dress code is being abandoned because their employees were abusing the privilege and coming to work in sloppy apparel; however, one thing remains constant: We definitely have a good idea of what is not professional. Also, what is appropriate for one industry or person may not be for another. Standards differ from profession to profession and industry to industry. For example, an automotive technician probably would not wear a pin-striped suit complete with vest and tie to apply for a job; likewise, a senior networking administrator or human resources manager would most certainly not show up for an interview in blue jeans. What is needed here are some general guidelines to use in determining what you should wear so you are seen as a professional in your field and you make a good first impression.

First impressions stay with an interviewer, and, like it or not, the clothes you wear create an image and play a major part in how you are perceived. Nemnich and Jandt say in their book *Cyberspace Job Search Kit*, "The amount of care you take in dressing appropriately for your job interview equates in an employer's mind with how much respect you have for the proffered job."[2] Consequently, if you wish to be treated as a professional, you must create a professional image, and this is determined, in a large part, by how you dress.

Color

One of the important aspects of your dress is the color you choose. Some colors convey a message of power or energy, some are interpreted negatively, and some convey a positive impression. The most desirable for an interview, quite obviously, would be colors that emphasize the positive.

Many people assume dark colors are always safe, but this is not always true. Black is a power color, and wearing a completely black outfit could intimidate your interviewer. Think about it: Who is always dressed in black? Judges, ministers, and, of course, people in mourning sometimes wear black. If black is your very best color, and it is the only thing you have to wear, add a brightly colored accessory to offset that authoritative tone. Blues are always safe colors, especially navy blue. Blues convey serenity and a sense of balance. Grays and burgundy are also considered to be good choices because they represent dignity. Brown is a very somber color and can project a mood of despondency, so again, if it is the only thing you have, give it a spot of cheer by adding another color. Pastels such as yellow, pink, and light blue do nicely as a contrast color but not as a total look.

Other colors that could convey the wrong message are green and yellow. Studies show that green and yellow are the least-liked colors of executives. In general, wear a color that looks good on you and one that isn't going to shock the interviewer.

Style

The second aspect of dressing professionally is the style of clothes you wear. *Conservative* is the key. For women, it is especially important to convey the image of someone who is serious about her career. Avoid frilly blouses, see-through materials, or "little girl" clothes. If you want to be taken seriously, you must dress seriously. Authors Greenleaf and Schaefer say, "While looking good is important, leave your sex appeal at home.[3] The key is to be attractive through class and attention to detail, not through revealing clothing. A simple suit or skirt and jacket is always a good choice. Women should wear closed shoes with medium-height heels and flesh-colored nylons. Men should avoid casual sportswear, faddish apparel, and sneakers, and your socks should be the same color, or a close match, to your suit or pants and jacket.

Jewelry should be worn sparingly and should be either gold, silver, or good-quality costume jewelry. Anything that dangles and is heavy makes you look as if you're going out for the evening. Many men today wear more jewelry than was formerly acceptable. This is more common than it was a decade ago, but some conservative companies in parts of the country still frown on this practice and do not view it as professional. Wearing it is certainly your decision, but when doing the research on the company with which you are interviewing, try to determine what would be acceptable. This is another good point for visiting the company beforehand to see what the employees are wearing. Obviously, multiple body piercings can be viewed as unacceptable when employees are required to greet and work with the public. Makeup and perfume can be inadvertently overdone, so moderation is essential. In addition to jewelry and perfume, your hairstyle is important as it is one of the first things people notice about you. For women, your cut should be one that complements the shape of your face. The same goes for men. Remember you are going to an interview, not on a date. Anything that could be labeled as "far out" can distract your interviewers and give them the opportunity to make assumptions that could hurt your chances of being offered the job.

An equally important factor in achieving a professional appearance is to choose apparel appropriate to the current season. Don't wear linens and lightweight fabrics in the winter or heavy woolens in the spring or summer. Cotton for shirts and blouses is a good selection year-round and always looks professional. White shoes, in most parts of the country, are not considered in good taste from September through April. The part of the country you live in has a definite bearing on what is appropriate. If you are new to the area and not sure what to wear, talk to a sales clerk in a well-known clothing store; he or she can usually give you some sound advice.

Don't observe what clothing the employees of the company for which you are interviewing are wearing and use that as a guideline except, as mentioned earlier, to observe the protocol for piercings and jewelry. It could be very misleading. They already have their jobs, so they are sometimes not concerned with the clothing they wear every day. Besides, everyone has "bad hair days" when they do not look their best. If it is a Friday, the employees might be wearing casual apparel if that is a custom at the company. However, interviewers want to know that *you* know how to dress professionally. After you get the job, you can wear what the others are wearing. Even then, if you are interested in being promoted, you might want to dress "up," that is, dress as if you already have that position. How you present yourself is one of the criteria on which many promotions are awarded. For additional tips for men and women, see the interview attire and grooming suggestions in the appendix.

Whether you're an automotive technician, a chief financial officer, or a graduate with a degree in business administration, the same rules apply: The employer is judging you as to how you would fit in as a potential representative of the company image.

How Interviews Are Conducted

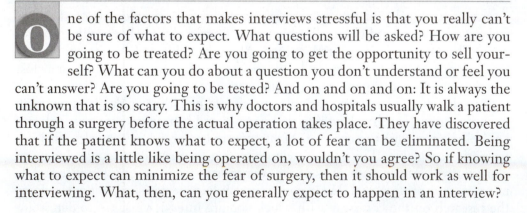

One of the factors that makes interviews stressful is that you really can't be sure of what to expect. What questions will be asked? How are you going to be treated? Are you going to get the opportunity to sell yourself? What can you do about a question you don't understand or feel you can't answer? Are you going to be tested? And on and on and on: It is always the unknown that is so scary. This is why doctors and hospitals usually walk a patient through a surgery before the actual operation takes place. They have discovered that if the patient knows what to expect, a lot of fear can be eliminated. Being interviewed is a little like being operated on, wouldn't you agree? So if knowing what to expect can minimize the fear of surgery, then it should work as well for interviewing. What, then, can you generally expect to happen in an interview?

Before the Interview

In most instances, you will be asked to complete an application form before interviewing. This is a very good reason to be early for the interview. If your interview

INTERVIEW DAY CHECKLIST

Use this checklist on the day of your interview.

○ 1. I have prepared a list of appropriate questions to ask the interviewer.

○ 2. I have my list of references ready should it be requested.

○ 3. I have reviewed my benefit statements and am prepared to sell myself to get the job.

○ 4. I have done the necessary research on the company where I'm interviewing.

○ 5. My hair is cut, washed, combed, and styled in a professional manner.

○ 6. I have bathed and used deodorant.

○ 7. My makeup, jewelry, and perfume or after-shave lotion are not excessive.

○ 8. My fingernails are trimmed, clean, and if polished, have been freshly done.

○ 9. My teeth are clean, and I have used a mouthwash for fresh breath.

○ 10. My shoes are clean, neat, and not scuffed.

○ 11. My clothes are clean, pressed, and styled appropriately for the job for which I'm interviewing. I feel comfortable in them.

○ 12. I promise myself that I will not fuss with or rearrange my clothing, hair, etc., once I arrive.

○ 13. I promise that I will be myself whatever the circumstances of the interview.

○ 14. I will take extra copies of resumes and transcripts, in case they ask for these. I will also bring my portfolio to assist me in selling my skills and abilities to the employer.

○ 15. I have all the necessary tools to complete the application form correctly and neatly should I be asked to fill one out.

---

time is set for 10 o'clock be there at least by 9:45. Also, your interviewer will love you for this, especially if he or she has finished with the one before you a little early. Interviewers are always eager to get on with the next one, and there you are, all ready to go! Being early also gives you time to check your notes and your appearance one last time before you meet your interviewer. It allows you to enter the interview relaxed and ready.

Many employers prefer to test an applicant before the interview, particularly in technical fields. Positions in electronics, mechanics, computer programming and networking, drafting, graphics, and word processing require levels of dexterity and accuracy that can be measured by performance tests or paper-and-pencil tests. Some employers evaluate prospective applicants through psychological testing (such as general intellectual ability and personality tests).

According to Caroline Hsu in *The Testing of America*, "Personality tests are increasingly a part of American life . . . and they are big business. The tests are being used in hiring, promotions, and professional development by a third of U.S. businesses . . . the online testing website *Tickle* administered 10 million personality tests."[4] There is one now being used in interviews and in the workplace, titled the Talent + interview (covered in the next section). The objective of psychological assessment is to obtain as pure an estimate as possible of characteristics such as intelligence, leadership potential, creativity, and so on. The downside of these tests is that they are highly controversial and widely criticized, not regulated by state and federal agencies, and very costly to the employer. However, Hsu quotes John Putzier, a performance consultant and author of the new book *Weirdos in the Workplace*, who "argues that personality testing can be enormously valuable, precisely because often what is revealed as a weakness may actually be a strength."[5] Whatever the type of testing the employer uses, make every attempt to find out if you are going to be tested before the interview; the best way is simply to ask. You don't need any surprises the day of your interview; your anxiety level will be high enough.

Types of Interviews

There are as many kinds of interviews as there are companies and interviewers because everyone does things a little differently. How an employer decides to administer the interview could vary from a personal face-to-face interview to videotaping an applicant to possibly a lunch or phone interview. Still, interviews can generally be categorized in five basic types: the *group* or *committee/panel* interview, the *unstructured* (discussion) interview, the *structured* (direct) interview, the *Gallup* interview, and the *stress interview*.

Sometimes the size of the company determines the kind of interview you will have. The larger the company, the more structured and extensive your interview is likely to be. Larger companies have personnel staff who are usually skillful and experienced at conducting interviews, whereas smaller companies usually lack personnel staff, and managers and supervisors conduct all interviews. When you interview with a manager or supervisor, you might find that you know more about interviewing than the person sitting behind the desk. Whatever you encounter, it is best that you leave the control of the interview in the hands of the interviewer. If you are too aggressive or come across as a know-it-all, you could be seen as a usurper, a person who likes to infringe on others' authority.

Group or committee interview

In a *group interview*, several people ask questions of the applicant; the interviewers could include those who will be your peers if you are hired. Sometimes, applicants are interviewed more than one at a time and are asked to react to one another rather than to the interviewer(s) so they can determine how well you function in a group or team setting. Make eye contact with, and speak to, each individual.

In a *committee/panel interview*, generally used for hiring for high-level positions, one candidate is interviewed by several interviewers. Group or committee/panel interviews can be somewhat intimidating, but they needn't be. Do expect that you will have less time to think about your answers, but take your time and try to establish a degree of rapport with everyone in the group. Do not feel pressured to be totally spontaneous. Keep your answers short and direct. You might want to ask yourself why you are being interviewed in this way. Does it mean you are going to have more than one boss?

Unstructured interview

The *unstructured interview* is rather informal. The person interviewing you will expect you to do most of the talking by asking broad questions and may respond only with "Yes?" or "Is that so?" This type of interview usually yields more information about the applicant's opinions and reactions. In this kind of interview, job seekers often talk themselves right out of a job offer. Remember to stay focused on facts about your ability to fill the position, your qualifications, and what you can do for the company. Don't let nervousness sidetrack you into talking about irrelevant topics or personal trivia. Now is when your portfolio can be very useful to sell yourself to the interviewer.

Structured interview

The *structured interview* is the most commonly used and involves a predetermined pattern of questions that will be asked. It is considered to be the most valid for employee selection because the questions are usually drawn directly from the job description. The drawback to this type of interview is that it does not allow you to exhibit your personality, communication skills, or other attributes.

Stress interview

The fourth kind of interview is the *stress interview*. It is designed intentionally to put you under stress so that your behavior and your responses and reactions can be observed. It is not often used, and when it is, the reason is usually because the position for which you are applying is a high-stress one. The reason could be merely that you are being interviewed by someone who enjoys watching others in the hot seat. If you find yourself in a stress interview, stay calm, cool, and collected. The interviewer may deliberately and frequently interrupt you, remain silent for long periods of time, or ask stressful and intimidating questions. Try not to take anything personally. Just answer as well as you can and keep in mind that you are being tested to see if you can handle stress. The *Gallup* interview, developed by the Gallup Organization and founded by Don Clifton, a psychology graduate, "uses interview techniques to highlight qualities which make people succeed in particular jobs.[6]

If you are applying for a job in another city and cannot meet with the interviewer in person, you could be asked to do a videotaped interview via a third party such as a career service agency. To prepare for facing a video camera, you might want to practice beforehand. Your nonverbal communication is especially critical in this type of interview because the camera picks up and clearly records your body language more than an interviewer might in a face-to-face interview. Speak slowly and clearly and show enthusiasm, but don't overdo it. An employer might also require a phone interview either because an in-person interview is not possible or because the person interviewing you wants to see how you respond to questions over the phone. It is very important to prepare for this interview just as you would for a one on one. In addition to regular interview preparation, review the telephone tips in Chapter 3.

Lunch interviews are usually more casual than interviews done in the office, but don't forget it is still an interview. Follow the person doing the interview in whatever manner he or she sets. Whether it is casual or professional, don't order messy foods or alcohol. Also, even where it is still allowed, it is wise not to smoke.

For all types of interviews, always do your homework beforehand, show self-confidence, and trust yourself to manage anything that comes up tactfully and professionally. Then, no matter how *they* rate you, *you* will know that you did your very best.

How Employers Evaluate You

The one thing you can be sure of in any interview is that you will be evaluated. During the interview, an unconscious evaluation is taking place, and after the interview, a formal evaluation is done.

There are no standardized evaluation or rating forms that all employers use. Each company evaluates its applicants differently, according to the needs of the company or the division for which you would be working. The following list will give you an idea of some of the things that employers say they observe when interviewing a prospective employee.

- Attitude
- Personal appearance
- Ability to communicate, orally and in writing
- Skills, ability to perform the job
- Self-confidence, poise
- Enthusiasm for the job and the company
- Criticism of past employers, coworkers
- Goals, self-motivation
- Willingness to do whatever is asked (overtime, additional training)
- School grades/attendance
- Educational requirements of the job
- Pre-employment testing
- Leadership potential

Overall, your level of self-confidence will be measured by the way in which you present yourself to the interviewer. How you dress and speak, your mannerisms, and the validity and content of your answers to questions will all influence the employer's evaluation. A study done at UCLA a few years ago revealed that the impact of a performance was based 7 percent on the words used, 38 percent on voice quality, and 55 percent on nonverbal communication. So do your research, prepare your answers to possible questions, and maintain a positive attitude; this will carry you through most interviews with a good rating.

What Employers Are *Really* Looking For

side from the technical, administrative, or management skills called for in the job description, what kinds of personal and interpersonal skills do employers look for? Frequently, applicants who have the best skills, education, and abilities are not hired. Quite often, the applicant who gets the job is the one who doesn't have quite all of the required experience or education. Wondering why this is the case, I began to question employers about their reasons for choosing one applicant over another. What would be the strongest selling points for their choice?

I discovered there is much more to winning the approval of the interviewer and getting the job than skills and education. Being chosen over other applicants has everything to do with your interpersonal skills, your personality, and how you conduct yourself in the interview. Employers are looking for the applicant who fits with the company and its culture. Many interviewers told me that they hired the person with whom they felt the most comfortable, the one they believed would be a good match for their employees. Of course, this person also had to have most of the qualifications for the job to even get the interview, but the candidate was hired because he or she was *liked*.

By the time you're in the interview, the employer usually knows about your employment background, education, and skill level. Now the interviewer will try to determine if you are compatible with the company. This is one time when the old saying "Opposites attract" does not apply: Employers are looking for someone who is *like* them. The decision to hire or not hire becomes very subjective, so the more you understand about what takes place in the interviewer's mind, what she is looking for or feeling about you, the better chance you have of getting the job. An excellent way to do this is to practice reading people so you can respond accordingly. What kinds of cues is the interviewer giving you? What kinds of body language is he or she exhibiting?

Interpersonal Skills

The employer is interested in the occupational skills you have (such as typing 65 words per minute, programming, networking, repairing computers, designing a building, or doing a blood analysis), but he wants to know other things about you as well. Can you take criticism and direction? Can you follow instructions? Are you a good team player? Are you flexible and adaptable? Can you communicate clearly? Can you handle change and conflict? Are you reliable, dependable, and responsible? Do you have initiative? Can you hit the ground running? Can you take on additional responsibilities? Can you demonstrate uncompromising integrity, professional ethics, and morals? Over the past few years, we have observed the flagrant abuse of authority and the complete lack of integrity by many of our nation's top senior-level executives, so employers are screening applicants for these most important traits. Most important, over and above performing the duties of the position, are you going to get along well with your coworkers and your supervisors? Are you able to work with others who have different values, work habits, and cultures than you? Research shows that approximately 78 percent of all terminations take place not because the employee didn't perform the job well but because he or she had difficulty with coworker/supervisor relationships.

Personality

The employer's subjective evaluation also includes a determination on the kind of personality you have. To learn how to respond to the needs of the interviewer, you need to learn more about yourself. Gaining an in-depth understanding of your personality style has enormous value in your career, and learning how to use this knowledge will make you more successful in your job search. How perceptive or creative are you? Do you have warmth and diplomacy? Are you self-confident? Depending on the culture (personality) of the company, how closely does your personality match that of the company's current and most valued employees? If the company is filled with outgoing and gregarious people, you might not be a good choice if you are generally quiet and reserved—and vice versa. The other side of this coin is that *you* probably would not be happy working there. Before you begin interviewing, go back and review the exercises you completed in Chapter 1 on your interests, wants, and needs, and re-read the information presented on employer testing, pages 121–122. What kind of personality do you have?

You may disagree with judgments of this kind, thinking it shouldn't matter what your personality is as long as you can do the job. But it does matter. In today's world of committees, teams, quality circles, and participative management, you must blend in and be cohesive with your coworkers and management. If you don't, you will not only be very uncomfortable and dissatisfied, you will not be a productive worker—and neither will the people who must work with you. Also, it is highly probable you will not stay long at the job. Enlightened management knows this, and so to avoid constant and expensive turnover of employees, they do everything they can to hire the "right" employee.

Are You a Match?

How does the company determine if you are a match? Do employers have a crystal ball? No, they just practice a little detective work, and they may have given you a personality test such as the Myers-Briggs Type. From your answers to the questions they ask and/or your scores on the tests, they can learn a lot about your personality and character. Questions such as the following can uncover things that your resume and cover letter don't tell them:

- Tell me about yourself.
- What kinds of things do you do for relaxation?
- What are the qualities that you consider necessary in a good supervisor?
- If you've ever had a disagreement with a former coworker or supervisor, how did you deal with it?

In addition, if your answers are in any way negative or derogatory, this might indicate you have difficulty in relating to others or that you may not function well as a team member. Likewise, if you are not prepared with well-thought-out answers, the interviewer could draw a negative conclusion about your reliability: Maybe you can't be relied on to be prepared in the workplace either.

Conduct in the Interview

General Guidelines

Some basic rules of behavior and appropriate conduct should be observed during an interview. Remember, everything you do and say is observed by the interviewer and is important. These guidelines may seem trivial, but whether you follow them or not can determine the success—or failure—of the interview.

- Do not take notes during the interview unless the interviewer asks you to do so or you ask permission to do so. (*Do* make notes immediately afterward while it is still fresh in your mind.) It is sometimes intimidating for the interviewer to see you taking down what he or she is saying. If the company does not hire you, they could fear being accused of discrimination based on some innocuous statement made in the interview.
- Remember your interviewer's name and use it when speaking to her during the interview. Refer to the person as Mr. or Ms. unless invited to use their first name.

- When introductions are made, do offer to shake hands, whether the interviewer is a man or a woman, and make it a firm handshake. Be careful of bone crushers! If your hands are prone to perspire, either use a moisture-absorbing powder or run them under cold water for a few minutes just before you go in to the interview. There is nothing more dampening to the interview than a wet, limp handshake. Pamela J. Holland and Marjorie Brody (2005) have covered all types of handshakes in their book, *Help! Was That a Career Limiting Move?* It is a good choice of something to read before you go to an interview.

- Do not smoke, chew gum, or drink anything in the interview. Even if a beverage or cigarette is offered, you are probably better off turning it down. Today, smoking is prohibited in almost all offices, chewing gum is very unprofessional, and trying to balance a drink while being interviewed is risky. The last thing you need is to spill something on yourself, or worse, their carpet.

- Wait for the interviewer to offer you a chair before you sit down.

- Present yourself as an honest person. Do not try to hide anything, and above all, *never, never lie!* It will only come back to haunt you later. A lie that you think you get away with during an interview could come up after you're hired and cause you to be dismissed. I've placed students who will call me four to five months later saying they were just fired and asked to clear their desks and leave because they had lied in the interview.

- Sell yourself! Your job as an interviewee is to sell your assets to the interviewer. If you wait expectantly for questions and dutifully answer them, you have done absolutely nothing to distinguish yourself from the other applicants. Remember what I've said earlier about taking this opportunity to present your portfolio to the interviewer. It is a good selling tool simply because it distinguishes you as a sincere, motivated, and professional individual.

- Bring the necessary paperwork that may be required: an extra resume, college credentials or transcripts, your Job Skills Portfolio, and a reference sheet. Do not load yourself down with unnecessary props, however.

- Show enthusiasm and sincerity.

- Close the interview using the suggestions given in the section in Chapter 5, "How to Close the Interview."

Body Language

A very important part of your conduct in the interview is your body language. Sometimes it's not what you say in an interview but what you do that reveals many things to the interviewer. Volumes have been written about **body language:** the nonverbal messages that your facial expressions, physical stance, and gestures convey to a listener. Evidence shows that body language plays a vital part in communication. Experts estimate that as much as 65 percent of communication is nonverbal. Some common types of body language, such as the position of the body, hand gestures, and facial expressions, can enhance or even contradict what you actually say.

Facial expressions

Eye contact is extremely important during the interview. Continually averting your eyes could be interpreted as a sign of guilt, lack of self-confidence, or even dishonesty. You don't want to stare either, so just glance away from time to time.

Your mouth also is a major silent communicator. Smiling too much conveys an unnatural message, and pursed lips can be a signal of disapproval or a sour personality. You can gauge what is too much or too little by watching your interviewer and responding accordingly. Avoid touching any part of your face or hair during the interview: It can indicate nervousness or insecurity.

Body gestures

Crossed arms can mean defensiveness, dissatisfaction, or simply that you've found a comfortable place for your hands. Because the meaning is ambiguous, it is best to keep your hands in your lap. The head tilted far up indicates superiority; if it's tilted down most of the time, you are giving a message of submission. A ramrod straight posture can signal inflexibility, and the other extreme, slouching in the chair, could be viewed as an indication of laziness or disinterest. The physical distance that you put between yourself and the interviewer is very important. Everyone has his or her space, and you should not invade it. Don't lean on the desk or get too close when you are speaking with the interviewer. You will know if you've crossed that boundary by watching the person's eyes and stance. If you are too close to someone, he or she will usually move backward in an attempt to gain personal space again.

Hand gestures

Try to keep from gesturing too much with your hands, because it can be distracting or irritating to the interviewer. Avoid clenched hands—the white knuckle look—because it can reveal anxiety or fear. If at all possible, keep your hands in your lap and certainly not in your pockets. Keep them away from your face, hair, and clothing. Straightening your clothing or hair can be viewed as sign that you are unsure of yourself.

Questions You Could Be Asked and How to Answer

There is no guaranteed way to determine exactly what questions are going to be used. All companies have specific needs and ask questions related to those needs. Some questions, however, are very likely to be asked and are worth taking the time to prepare for. Some questions can be very difficult to answer extemporaneously. If you are not prepared with appropriate answers, you could be eliminated.

Here is a story about a young man who applied for a job that involved operating a small train station along a remote section of the track. The personnel officer of the train company interviewed him carefully to find out his qualifications. Then the officer said, "Well, it looks like you have the basic qualifications for the job, but we need somebody who can think on his feet and solve problems if they come up. Can you do that?" The young man replied, "Well, I think so." The personnel officer then said, "Okay, I'll give you a hypothetical problem concerning train operations, and you tell me how you'd solve it. Suppose you find out one day there's a southbound train headed down the only track that runs by your station. You also find out there's a northbound train coming up the same track. The engineers of the two trains don't know about each other. What would you do?"

The applicant replied, "I'd get on the telephone and call the stations down the track to notify them of the problem." Said the interviewer, "What would you do if you found out the telephone didn't work?" "Well," said the young man, "I'd use the telegraph." "Suppose the telegraph didn't work either?" "In that case," said the young man, "I'd run outside and throw the switch so that one of the trains would be shunted off onto the spur." The personnel officer said, "And what would you do if the switch was jammed?"

"Well, in that case I'd run home and fetch my brother." This left the interviewer somewhat puzzled, so he asked, "Why would you go home and get your brother?" To this, the young man replied, "Because he ain't never seen a train wreck before."

All joking aside, you do need to be prepared before tackling the interview process. The following 26 questions are likely to arise in interviews. Rehearse the questions and become very familiar with your qualifications so that you can show the employer how you can benefit the company.

1. *Tell me about yourself.* What does the interviewer want to know? That you took lessons in knitting or home improvement? Hardly. He is not looking for personal information. Don't begin by saying you are single or married, you have X number of children, or you are looking for a job with security. Take this opportunity to present your key qualities and your interest in and understanding of the company; focus on the needs of the company and its people, not what *you* want in a job. Don't be tempted to rattle off your employment history. This is the opportune time to sell yourself, to use some of the benefit statements you have written.

2. *What do you see yourself doing three (or five) years from now?* This question helps the interviewer determine if you plan ahead or just live from day to day. She wants to know if you have goals. If you have never before set goals and written them out, now is the time to do so. Preferably, your answer should relate to a possible career with their company. This is also the perfect opportunity to ask about the career path for this position. If you've done your research, you should have a pretty good idea of where you want to go with your career. Do not say you want to be in management without stating exactly what kind of management. So many people say this, thinking that it shows planning for the future; believe me, it does not. It just puts you in a category with those who have not done their homework.

3. *Which is more important to you, the money or the type of job you do?* With this question the interviewer attempts to find out whether you are "paycheck oriented." Be honest; explain that you, like everyone else, have to be concerned with the salary you receive because you have to support yourself (and your family, if that is the case), but that you also want a job you enjoy doing. Some applicants make the mistake of answering this question by saying that money is not important to them. Usually, this will only lead the employer to believe you will take a low salary.

4. *How would you describe yourself?* This is a tricky question, so be careful how you answer it. The interviewer is asking you to describe yourself in terms other than "I'm 28 years old; I have a degree in business administration," and so on. She is looking for information about your personality, your character, and what kind of worker you are. This is a good place to mention your functional skills, flexibility, communication, and responsibility.

5. *What is your greatest weakness (or strength)?* Most job seekers are completely stumped by this question because they have never taken the time to consider

their weaknesses or strengths. Also, some people find it very difficult to talk about themselves. As with all questions, avoid giving personal answers. An appropriate answer would be to mention one of your work-related weaknesses or strengths. Are you a workaholic or too detail oriented? Does your strength lie in the fact that you get along well with coworkers or that you have excellent communication skills? These are the kinds of qualities interviewers look for. If you describe a weakness, mention as well that you are aware of the weakness and are working on correcting it.

6. *What motivates you to put forth your greatest effort?* Employers know that to obtain the most productivity from their employees, they must offer motivation. When the employer knows what motivates you, she can provide you with greater job satisfaction, and in turn will have a more productive worker. Are you motivated by money, rewards, recognition, responsibility, self-satisfaction? Think about this before you interview and prepare an answer in case you are asked. (For help, review the section on values in Chapter 1.)

7. *Why should I hire you?* What the interviewer really wants to know is "How are you different from the others who have applied for this position?" If you are unable to sell yourself because you don't know the answer to this question, you could lose the job offer. Your research should have given you some information about the company and what they are looking for in an employee. Remember that all companies are looking for people who can help them make a profit. Show the employer you have qualities that can help to save time and make money, and you have just provided a reason to hire you. Now is the perfect opportunity to use your benefit statements and your portfolio. Be specific! Can you increase productivity, cut expenses, and build good customer relations?

8. *Why are you leaving your present job? Why did you leave your last job?* Stress reasons that put you in the best light, such as that you need more room for growth and advancement. Above all, *do not criticize your present or past supervisor or employer.*

9. *How do you feel about relocating?* Unless you absolutely do not want to relocate, or can't because of personal reasons, you can say you are open to discussing relocating at the appropriate time. Things change, and it's always a possibility that, at a later date, you might want to relocate.

10. *What salary do you expect?* In the first interview, try to avoid this subject and do not ask about salary yourself. James E. Challenger, president of Challenger, Gray & Christmas, Inc., an outplacement firm, advises applicants not to bring up the subject of money in the first interview because it sends a message that you are more interested in yourself than in the job. However, if it is asked, you need to be prepared with an answer without locking yourself into a set figure. Answer that you believe the salary should be commensurate with your ability to perform the job and to contribute to the firm's goals, and you would like to wait to discuss salary when you have the details of what the job entails. If you are pressed for an answer, never give a single figure; always give a salary range and add that you are willing to negotiate.

11. *Do you smoke, drink, or use drugs?* If at all possible, avoid any emotional reaction to this question. Whether you do, have, or never have, it almost always gets an emotional reaction. To some interviewers, this could signal guilt. An employer can legally ask questions of this nature and require pre-employment drug and

alcohol testing as long as the reason is to determine whether an applicant can regularly and successfully perform the job for which the employer is hiring. If this question is asked, do not try to avoid answering. Just be prepared to give an honest answer.

12. *What do you do to reward yourself after a difficult and stressful day or week?* Employers are interested in whether you are able to relax and to lead a balanced life. Because they cannot ask this directly because it is personal, they get the information by asking this question. They also want to know if you are pursuing additional education or training, or are an active, industrious person. Let's face it, you might be considered a not-too-motivated person if you sit in front of the television set from Friday through Sunday.

13. *I see you're not married. Do you live with a man (or woman)? Do you plan to have children? Do you have adequate child care?* It is illegal for an interviewer to ask any of these questions. As with all illegal questions, ask politely if this has a bearing in any way on your ability to perform the job. Or you could reply that you are willing to answer any questions about your skills and qualifications to perform the job and ask if this is required information for the job. You also might ask yourself at this time whether you would want to work for a firm that is so insensitive and ignorant as to permit questions of this nature. As to reporting them, go ahead if you want to, but remember the burden of proof is on you. It will be your word against the interviewer's, and the EEOC requires proof to prosecute.

14. *Have you ever been fired or asked to resign?* This is a legitimate question, but a very sensitive one, and how you answer could mean the difference between getting and not getting a job offer. If you have been fired, the most appropriate answer is, "Yes, I have, and as I look back on it, I realize that I could have done things differently. I learned a lot about myself from that experience." Then stop, and don't say any more unless you are asked for details. I've found that 95 percent of the time, you won't be. You probably have given the needed information, that *you take responsibility for your role in that termination.* Never bad-mouth a former employer or supervisor. You will not be hired if you do. No one wants to deal with an employee who is insubordinate, blames others for what happens, and does not accept responsibility for his or her actions.

15. *Why do you want to work for us?* "I don't know" or "I need a job" are not exactly the best answers. Your goal should be to convince the interviewer that this company is the one you really want to work for. You can do this by saying you are sold on the company's product or service, or that from your research, you found the company is employee-oriented and offers opportunities for growth and advancement. Of course, you must do your research so you have a factual answer, not a glib statement.

16. *How good is your health?* The interviewer is treading on thin ice with this question (see the section on legal and illegal questions later). You can answer it by saying that nothing about your health will prevent you from doing the job for which you are applying.

17. *I don't believe you have enough experience for this position.* Now is the best time to sell your functional skills, and if it is possible for you to do so, offer to begin at a little lower salary with the opportunity to prove yourself in a given period of time. You might want to ask for more information about the job: "What would

a typical day in this position require? What would I be doing?" Get specifics, and then use this information to show that your skills are appropriate. Most important, do not be defensive or argumentative; be agreeable, but sell yourself *with other qualities.* The objective is to persuade the interviewer you can do the job and you are able to learn quickly. If you've just graduated from college, stress the fact that in school you had hands-on or practical experience in the skills, if your college did provide you with a self-paced, work-simulated environment to prepare you for the actual workplace. You can add that because you just came from a learning environment, you can be trained quickly, thereby saving the company time and money. Point out that you are perfectly capable of learning from a manual if one is available.

18. *I see you've been out of the job market for several years; do you believe your skills are still up to date?* This question is usually directed to people returning from parental leaves, schooling, or sabbaticals. Focus on the knowledge and experience you gained through home study or research, volunteer work, schooling, and home projects. Inform the interviewer that although you were not employed for a salary, you have been continually learning and improving your skills. Stress that you learn quickly and you would be willing to take whatever courses or training is needed to upgrade your skills. As with the previous question, suggest you are capable of learning from an instruction manual or tutorial, which saves time and money.

19. *Have you met your military obligations? Are you currently serving in the National Guard?* The first question is illegal and not relevant unless a draft is in place. The second one is legal, and if you are in the National Guard, just assure the interviewer that your service is not going to interfere with your ability to perform the job. Obviously, in times when the country is at war, your answer needs to be appropriately relevant to what your honest status is at the time.

20. *Of all the jobs you've held, which one did you like the most? The least? Why?* Interviewers ask questions like this to determine if the work environment is suitable for you. Be careful not to mention reasons that would conflict with the environment or the duties of the job. Formulate your answer around general work-related responsibilities and avoid specifics. This can also present an excellent opportunity for you to ask questions about their environment.

21. *If you are hired, how long do you plan to stay with our company?* I've heard a lot of career counselors tell job seekers to answer "Forever." Both you and the interviewer know this is very unlikely to be true, so don't say it. An appropriate and honest answer is simply to say you will stay as long as it's mutually beneficial. According to research by Walker Information Global Network, a workplace consulting firm, the average employee has 12 to 15 jobs during his or her lifetime and stays with a job an average of 3.6 years.[7]

22. *Can you work under pressure or deadlines?* If you can and are willing to do so, give examples from your background that demonstrate your ability to handle stress, pressure, and so on. Be sure to include *how* you handled it.

23. *How do you feel about working for a female (male) boss?* Caution! This is a loaded question and could put a noose around your neck. The only correct answer is to say either would be fine, that gender is not an issue but it is the management or supervisory ability of the person that matters.

24. *What immediate contribution can you make to our company?* The keyword in this question is "immediate"; very few employees make an immediate contribution to any company. New employees always have some downtime: time to train and just to get familiar with the company. So, be honest and say this, but add that after this period, you will contribute to the company by being an industrious and reliable employee. Illustrate this with one of your benefit statements. You have probably discovered what the company's needs are from your research, so you can state some specific contributions you can make based on that information.

25. *Do you have any questions?* This is usually the last question of the interview, and unless the interviewer has completely covered everything, you should have some relevant questions to ask. Remember, *don't ask about salary, benefits, or things of this nature*. You're probably dying to know so you can decide if this job is for you, right? But, unless you have been made an offer, you don't have a decision to make at this time.

26. *Are you interviewing with anyone else?* This is not exactly a professional question because the interviewer is asking for information that he really has no right to. However, because you don't want to ignore it or not answer, you could say, "Yes, I am. I realized when I began my job search that I should market my skills to as many companies as I could. This will enable me to choose the one best suited to my job goals."

Behavioral Screening Questions

Over the past few years, behavioral interviewing, also known as competency-based interviewing, has become a popular method with many companies for selecting candidates. The idea behind behavioral interviewing is that the candidate's past performance is the most accurate for determining future performance. Some interviewers use a method called **behavioral screening,** asking questions that deal with actual past experiences in specific situations. When an interviewer asks this kind of question, she is looking for a brief description of a specific problem or situation, what you did about it, and what were the results. The interviewer does not want to hear your opinion or how you deal with things in general. Do not respond to the questions in the future tense, that is, what you *would do* if faced with a particular situation. Before you respond to this kind of question, take your time to think about your answer. You don't have to answer immediately. This kind of question gives you the opportunity to sell yourself, so take advantage of it. To prepare for a behavioral interview, prepare some statements in advance about previous experiences when you, for example, dealt effectively with stress, showed initiative in your job, worked cooperatively and successfully in a team, demonstrated proficient customer service skills, or had a failure in your job and how you overcame it. Here are a few examples of behavioral screening questions:

1. Give me an example of a time when you needed to adjust to a situation quickly. What did you do, and how did it turn out?

2. Tell me about a situation when you had to stand up for a decision you made even though it was unpopular.

3. What has been your experience in working with conflicting, delayed, or ambiguous information? What did you do to make the most of the situation?

4. Solving a problem often necessitates evaluating alternate solutions. Give me an example of a time when you actively defined several solutions to a single problem. Did you use any tools such as research or brainstorming?

5. The correct understanding of differences in personality can affect work decisions such as work assignments, employee motivation, and conflict management. Tell how your knowledge of personality differences has benefited your effectiveness.

Dealing with Difficult Questions

Sometimes in an interview you are asked questions for which you may not feel you have an answer. To deal with these, first be sure you clearly understand the question. Ask the interviewer to repeat or rephrase it for you, or ask for examples. Encourage the interviewer to tell you more by asking specific questions. If you still are not sure how to answer, ask for a few minutes to think it over, or ask if you can come back to it. If you simply do not know the answer, say so. It is far better to admit not knowing than to give an answer that makes a fool of you. Some interviewers ask questions that they are fairly certain you cannot answer to see if you will try to bluff your way through them. This could indicate to them that you would do the same on the job, which could cause accidents, poor-quality workmanship, and unhappy customers. Remember, no one has all the answers.

Additional Interview Questions

Following are more questions you might encounter during interviews. To prepare, think about how you would answer them.

1. How do you feel about your present job?
2. How many hours do you feel a person should devote to a job?
3. What are some of the things about which you and your former supervisor(s) have disagreed?
4. What kind of people do you like working with? What kind do you find difficult to work with?
5. What are some of the things you would like to avoid in a job? Why?
6. How would you describe a good supervisor?
7. Which one of your accomplishments has given you the most satisfaction?
8. Do you have reliable transportation to and from work?
9. What one thing do others need to know about you to work effectively with you?
10. How do you define success?
11. What was your most rewarding experience in college?
12. Why did you choose this career?
13. What have you learned from your mistakes?
14. Are you planning to continue your education?
15. Are you willing to spend three to six months as a trainee?
16. Do you work better in a team or by yourself?
17. Have you changed careers in the past year?
18. If you were hiring a person for this position, what skills and abilities would you look for?

Your Turn to Question

You can demonstrate your interest in the company and prior research by asking pertinent and intelligent questions of your interviewer. Answers to these questions will give you a clearer picture of how the company's objectives relate to your interests and assist you in making a decision about a job offer. Beware, however, of asking too many questions, and watch your interviewer for signals (such as looking at a watch) that the interview is over. Consider these suggestions for questions you could ask:

1. Can I answer any questions about my qualifications for this position?

2. Would you please describe the job duties for me? Do you have a copy of the job description I could see?

3. Do you have a formal training program? How long is it? Please describe it.

4. Is this a newly created position?

5. What type of education and experience do you most like to find in persons filling this position?

6. Was the person who previously held this job promoted?

7. Will I be responsible for supervising other staff? If so, how many?

8. How do you evaluate your employees? How often?

9. Could you describe a typical career pathway in your organization for an employee in this position?

10. How does today's economic environment affect your organization?

11. Do you have plans for expansion in terms of product development, services, new branch offices, etc.?

12. From your experience, what would you say are the company's greatest strengths?

13. How do you rate your competition?

14. What is your employee turnover rate?

15. Would you say that your company follows a chain-of-command-type management policy or one of a less structured, participative nature similar to MacGregor's theory Y? (You may not want to use this question unless you have some basic understanding of management theories.)

16. How much involvement do your employees have in making decisions or setting policies and procedures?

17. How long have you been with this company, and what about it do you like best?

18. Will there be any further testing?

19. Will I be required to take a physical examination?

20. When will you be making your decision as to whom you're going to hire? May I call you on_____?

Questions Not to Ask

1. *Is this a union shop?* You should already know this from your research. It can also be a very threatening question to the interviewer if the company is not. You might be suspected of being a union organizer.

2. *What happened to the person who had this job before?* You are asking for personal information, and the question could sound antagonizing. Instead, rephrase it. See questions 4 and 6 in the preceding list.

3. *Will I have to work much overtime?* The interviewer will see you as a time-clock puncher.

4. *How much job security do you offer?* Job security is a myth—don't even mention it. Helen Keller said, "Security is mostly a superstition. It does not exist in nature, nor do the children of men, as a whole, experience it." This has never been more true than it is today with mergers, takeovers, outsourcing, and the total reorganization of many companies. Your security comes from within you.

5. *When will I get my first salary raise?* This question is totally inappropriate until you have been offered the position and have accepted.

6. *What is it that you people do at this company?* Believe it or not, applicants actually ask this question. Obviously, if you have to ask this, you are not in the running for the position. Do your homework so you know this before the interview.

7. *Can you afford me?* This question conveys a message of arrogance and over-confidence. It could be very insulting to the interviewer.

8. *What kind of benefits do you offer?* Any question related to salary or compensation, including benefits, is not appropriate until you have been made a job offer.

9. *If I'm asked to relocate, will the company pay for it?* You're assuming that you're going to get the job, so it is a premature question.

10. *How many people are you interviewing?* The answer to this question should really not be of concern to you. It might lead the interviewer to think that you are insecure or just plain nosy.

Legal and Illegal Pre-Employment Questions

The Equal Employment Opportunity Commission and two federal laws, the Civil Rights Act of 1991 and the employment provisions of the Americans with Disabilities Act of 1990, govern the questions that may be asked on application forms and in interviews. Employers who ask illegal questions leave themselves open to charges of bias and lawsuits. Read the following list to be aware of questions you do not have to answer.

- *Name:* It is legal to ask, for access purposes, whether the applicant's work records are under another name. It's illegal to ask if a woman is Miss, Ms., or Mrs. and to request the applicant to give a maiden name or any other name he or she has used. (Legislation: Title VII as amended by Equal Employment Opportunity Title IX.)

- *Address/housing:* It's legal to request a current address and phone number and how the applicant can be contacted if a phone number is not available. It is illegal to ask for past residences, length of residence at a particular address, and whether applicant owns or rents. (Legislation: Title VII.)

- *Age:* It is legal to ask age *only* if it is needed to show that an applicant is old enough to work or serve alcohol. It's illegal to request a birth certificate or similar records showing age. (Legislation: Age Discrimination Act of 1967.)

- *Race/color:* Any inquiry about color or race is illegal unless it is done under the Affirmative Action program. (Legislation: Title VII.)

- *Sex:* Again, inquiries may be made only under an Affirmative Action program. The question is legal when it is job related, (e.g., when hiring locker room or rest-room attendants). (Legislation: Title VII and IX.)

- *Religion/creed:* There are no legal questions about religion or creed, religious customs, or holidays. (Legislation: Title VII.)

- *Marital/parental status:* Employers may ask these questions only after hiring and only for insurance purposes. It is illegal to ask questions of any nature regarding children, who cares for them, or if the applicant plans to have them. (Legislation: Title IX and VII.)

- *Relatives:* After hiring, employers may ask for the name, relationship, and address or phone number of a person to be notified in case of an emergency. Nepotism policies that have a disparate impact on one sex are illegal. (Legislation: Title IX.)

- *Military service:* It is legal to inquire about job-related experience in the U.S. Armed Forces but illegal to request information on the type of discharge or for military service records.

- *Education:* Employers can ask about job-related education and English-language skills only if they are required for the work to be performed. Questions about nationality or racial or religious affiliation of schools attended are illegal, as are inquiries as to how a foreign language ability was acquired. (Legislation: Title VII.)

- *Criminal records:* It is illegal to ask for arrest records involving no subsequent conviction. (Legislation: Title VII.)

- *Organizations:* It is legal to ask about organizational and professional affiliations that are job related so long as the information is not used to discriminate on the basis of race, color, etc. (Legislation: Title VII.)

- *Photographs:* After hiring, it is legal to request photos for identification or security purposes. (Legislation: Title VII.)

- *Work schedules:* It is legal to ask about willingness to work required schedules but not to work specific religious holiday(s). (Legislation: Title VII.)

- *Physical data:* It is illegal to require applicants to give height and weight or other nonspecified, non-job-related physical data. It is legal to ask applicants to prove their ability to do manual labor, lifting, and other physical requirements for the safe performance of the job. (Legislation: Title VII.)

- *Handicap(s):* It is legal to inquire about physical handicaps for the purpose of determining the applicant's capability to perform the job. (The burden of proof lies with the employer for nondiscrimination.) It is illegal to exclude applicants with disabilities on the basis of their type of disability. (Each case must be determined on an individual basis by law.) (Legislation: Americans with Disabilities Act, Handicap Discrimination Guidelines of the Revised Code, Chapter 4112.)

- *National origin/citizenship:* All employers are required to have applicants (after hiring) complete the Employment Eligibility Verification (Form I-9), which is proof of citizenship or "intending citizen" (an alien who has been lawfully admitted to the United States). (Legislation: IRCA of 1986, EEOC, Title VII.)

Other questions that employers are advised to avoid are the following:

- Graduation date from grade school, high school, or college.
- Diseases or major illnesses for which the applicant has been treated.
- Hospitalization history, including mental health treatment.
- Prescription drugs being taken.
- Past treatment for drug addiction or alcoholism.
- Workers' compensation history.
- Whether applicant has ever filed for bankruptcy.
- Past garnishment of wages.

Guidelines on closing the interview, negotiating for salary and benefits, and keeping your job after you're hired are covered in Chapter 5.

NOTES

1. Mary B. Nemnich and Fred E. Jandt, *Cyberspace Job Search Kit 2000–2001 Edition: The Complete Guide to Online Job Seeking and Career Information* (Indianapolis, IN: JIST Publishing, 2001), 74–76. Reprinted by permission.

2. Ibid., p. 215.

3. Clinton T. Greenleaf III and Stefani Schaefer, *Attention to Detail: A Woman's Guide to Professional Appearance and Conduct* (Chesterland, OH: Greenleaf Enterprises, 2000), 12.

4. Caroline Hsu, "The Testing of America," *U.S. News & World Report* (September 20, 2004), 67. Copyright U.S. News & World Report, L.P. Reprinted by permission.

5. Caroline Hsu, "Science & Society," *U.S. News & World Report* (September 20, 2004), 68. Copyright U.S. News & World Report, L.P. Reprinted by permission.

6. Standard Life Investments, Limited.com, *Gallup Interviews.* Accessed on April 11, 2008.

7. Walker Global Network, www.walkerinfo.com/globalnetwork.

Closing the Job Search Process

Closing the interview process can be an unnerving

experience unless you prepare for this the same as

the other parts of the interview. You want to close

on a positive note and be certain you have received

and provided all the required information to help

you make a decision if offered the job.

CHAPTER

5

Getting and Keeping the Job

How to Close the Interview

If you have done the proper research, you should already have a good idea of what the company is looking for and whether those requirements match your needs in a job. As mentioned earlier, you should not take notes during the interview, but it is okay to check notes you've made before the interview to determine if you have the information you need and the information you want the interviewer to have. When you are being interviewed, you let the person doing the interview take charge—up until the close, that is. During the interview, you do not interrupt, disagree with, or contradict your interviewer (even if it appears that he or she is inexperienced and handling the interview rather badly). You can, however, influence how you are judged by the way you answer the questions, by being aware of your body language, and by the questions you ask. Now, at the close of the interview, it is especially important that you get the information you need, so you should subtly and professionally exercise some control.

When you are asked if you have any questions, that's a signal the interview is winding down. After you have asked your questions, you have the opportunity to make some important points. First, be sure to reiterate your strong points for the position; then ask if the interviewer has any questions about your qualifications. Finally, ask these questions: When will a decision be made? Will you be contacted, or would it be appropriate for you to contact the interviewer? When would be the best time to call? Will there be second or third interviews? Will you be tested? The interviewer may not remember to tell you all these things, so ask now.

Always end the interview by reaffirming your interest in the job and thanking the interviewer for taking the time to consider you for the position. Many employers have told me they hire the person who asks for the job, so do emphasize your interest in the company and the position.

Follow-up After the Interview

When the interview is over, you wipe your brow, breathe a sigh of relief, and head for the nearest bar for a beer, right? Of course not! One of the first things you do is to find a quiet place and make some notes about the interview. How did you feel during the interview? Did you promise to provide more information if it was needed? If so, when? Did you forget to tell them something you felt would reinforce your credibility to do the job? Make a reminder to include it in your thank-you letter. Did you forget to ask something? Make yourself a note to ask when you call. Keeping records of and evaluating all interviews will help you to remember what took place, and later, to be able to make a sound decision as to an offer if one is made. You should also assess your performance by completing the Post-Interview Self Evaluation form in the appendix. Take the time to reexamine your qualifications and your weak points. This time to recap is so important because after many interviews, the facts and your feelings will tend to blur. Don't trust your memory; jot it down.

After you've made your notes and done your evaluation, the last but most important follow-up to all interviews is to send a thank-you letter. A thank-you letter is a brief, well-written reminder that you are the best person for the job. Go back to Chapter 2 and review the suggestions on how to compose your thank-you letters. Whether you want the job or not, and regardless of how the interview went, always send a thank-you to your interviewer(s). Send separate ones to each of your interviewers if there were more than one. As mentioned earlier, some hiring decisions have been made on this point alone.

One final note about follow-up: Even if you don't get the job, follow the rejection with a response. You can either call or write a short letter expressing your appreciation for the time spent with you and asking that you be considered for future openings when they arise. Sending a letter is best because job seekers do not often do it, so it sets you apart from your competition. Applicants who were turned down for the first position have often been called for a second one. In addition, if you were offered the job but turned it down, write a polite letter thanking the company for offering you the position and give valid reasons for declining. You want to keep your options open for future opportunities. *Note*: For assistance in writing all follow-up letters, review the instructions in Chapter 2.

What to Do Between Interviews

When you are looking for employment, you need to devote as much time to it as possible. If you are unemployed, treat job hunting as though it were your job, giving it eight hours a day and no less than five days a week. If you are looking while you are holding a full-time job, you need to use all available time you have before and after work, during lunch hours, and on Saturdays. Many employers will meet with you on their lunch hour, after work, or on Saturday if you've given them good reason to do so—that is, if you've created a desire in them to consider you for a position they have open. The only way to acquire the job you want is to pursue it with all the energy, commitment, and determination you can muster. That means that you continue to search out job leads and openings and to arrange for interviews when you are between interviews. You do not sit by the phone waiting to hear from an interviewer who "almost promised" you the job. Remember from Chapter 3, it took persons looking for work in 2007 3.6 months to find a job. I assure you, you can shorten that length of time if you pursue your search seriously and diligently.

Job seekers very often come back to me from an interview absolutely *positive* that they had the job because "the interviewer just the same as said so." Well, many times they didn't have it. Most interviewers are very positive during the interview and will give you strong indications that you are "the one." This may be because they do have an interest in you, and they want you to hold your options open for them *in case* they decide to offer you the job. Interviewers are also sometimes very inept at rejecting applicants face to face. Or it may be that at the time you were interviewed, you were the best applicant, but a subsequent interview may have produced another applicant who was better qualified. So don't sit around waiting for a call. If you don't get the job, you are back to square one. You will have to get your momentum and morale up and your feelings of rejection down. So don't waste time sitting by the phone and checking the mailbox when you could be generating new job leads and interviews. The strongest argument in favor of keeping busy with your job search while you wait to hear is that your feelings of rejection will be minimized if you have another interview or offer pending when you get the "Sorry" call or letter.

Dealing with Rejection

Realistically, it is very rare that you get the first job for which you interview. Prepare yourself to accept the fact that you will have to deal with some rejection. Everyone I've ever known, including your author, has had difficulty dealing with rejection. We often assume there is something wrong with us, when in fact, there isn't. Ninety-nine percent of the time, rejection says nothing about you but more about the person who is doing the rejecting. In a job search, being rejected can be devastating unless you prepare yourself to handle it constructively. Here are some tips to help you.

Above all, don't take it personally

Rejection has nothing to do with you as a person. The chances are you didn't get the job because you didn't fit with the company because of some minor detail. If the employer didn't feel you would fit in with the other employees, you probably *wouldn't* have. This can be a blessing in disguise because had you gotten the job, the possibility is very strong you would not have felt comfortable and would have quit soon after taking it. That just wasn't the right job for you; yours is still out there waiting for you.

Find others who are job searching

Either join a job search support group or establish one of your own. In many cities, the employment section of your local newspaper publishes lists of activities, workshops, and support groups for all kinds of people looking for work. If you are a recent graduate and your college has a job placement office, check with the counselors who are in charge to determine if they offer a support group of other graduates who are also looking for a job. There is a lot to be gained from getting and giving help and support to others who are facing the same situation as you. You can give each other moral support and encouragement and exchange ideas about what works or doesn't work. You may even get job leads—all job seekers, when they are searching, uncover positions that do not apply to them.

Don't get sidetracked

This is not the time to clean the garage or the hall closet, or to change the oil in your car. Devote your energy to finding a job. It is tempting to want a reprieve from the rigors of job searching; however, you could lose out on interviews and/or job offers while you are involved with those diversions. You also lose your momentum and stimulation which is definitely needed in a job search endeavor.

Do your own footwork

Don't sign up with an agency unless you have exhausted all possibilities. Even then, be very cautious because you are very vulnerable at this time and may be tempted to take a job that is not right for you. Besides, you have all the techniques right in this book that agencies use to find jobs, maybe even more. Make more cold calls and get more information on what you are qualified to do and for which companies. The more you know about what employers are looking for in your field, the better you can sell yourself to them. Also, you could reap a double reward from this: In the process of getting information, you could acquire viable job leads.

Don't turn down any interview

Even if the job looks like one that you wouldn't be particularly interested in, you just never know what might turn up. Also, the more you interview, the better you become at selling yourself. In addition, all companies have associates and others with which they interact, and there is always a sharing of information about job openings they have. That could mean a referral for you if they know someone who is looking for a person with your skills.

Look at your job search as a positive learning experience

Every time you interview, get turned down, or talk to an employer about a job, you learn more about yourself and your capabilities. Keep an open mind and be willing to analyze the feedback you're getting from others.

Job searching is sometimes simply a "numbers game"

According to the law of averages, after so many calls, interviews, and "no's," you are bound to get a "yes." So just keep going! As with any undertaking in life, there are usually some setbacks, some losses before you are successful.

Evaluating the Job Offer and Negotiating Salary

I received a phone call one day from a former student I had placed in an excellent position with a prestigious company. Julie said that it was a very good job, the employer was very good to her, and she was making more than an adequate salary, but she just wasn't happy. She said, "Carolyn, I need to come talk to you; this job is just not what I want. There is no challenge, and I'm not using the talents that I know I have. I guess I just didn't look at the job closely enough before I took it." Sound familiar?

This can happen to you if you don't take the time to evaluate the job and the company in relation to your abilities and goals. You may become like the workers that Fredrick Herzberg, noted psychologist and professor at Case Western Reserve University, speaks of in his book *Work and the Nature of Man*. He says that most workers are in a sort of neutral world, neither satisfied nor dissatisfied. Do you doubt this? I challenge you—survey offices in any city in the United States and observe how many workers display signs, posters, or pictures that say "Hang in there, it's only Monday," "I'd rather be fishing/camping/skiing," or "T.G.I.F. (Thank God It's Friday!)." Robert G. Allen, author of *Creating Wealth*, echoes the bumper sticker that reads "I owe, I owe, so it's off to work I go!" when he says that 20 million+ people go off to work each day to jobs they can't stand because they value security more than satisfaction. This number increases when the availability of jobs becomes scarce.

How can you avoid being one of those 20 million? By taking the time to seriously consider the self-assessments you completed in Chapter 1 and comparing them to the job *before* you accept it. Evaluating a job offer is the final step in successful job searching and the key to job satisfaction. Many applicants accept jobs that are not right for them. After all, you've worked hard at doing all the "right" things to get interviews, and now you finally have an offer. You should eagerly accept it, right? You can usually think of a thousand reasons why you should take it, but unfortunately, you probably haven't considered the reasons why perhaps you shouldn't. Often the only thing job searchers consider when given a job offer is the salary, and even then they usually accept less than what they are worth.

Only when you have matched the job offer to your self-assessment can you be certain that it is the right job for you. The "ideal job" is a match of several factors, not just the salary and benefits. If those factors are present, *only then* is it appropriate to examine the salary and benefits.

Negotiating Your Salary

Before you attempt to negotiate with an employer for a salary, you must be certain that a solid job offer has been made. Once this has been established and you've decided you want the job, the next step—*before* you speak with the employer—is to learn as much as you can about how companies set salaries. Many factors determine the salary a company offers a prospective employee. A company may use different means to set their salary offer: The Job Worth system (sometimes called the Factor Comparison Method), the Market Worth system, the salaries of other employees within the company, the company's ability to pay, market demand, and sometimes, your last or current salary.

In the Job Worth system, each job in the company is assigned a point value. Points are awarded on the basis of the following criteria:

- Job responsibilities
- Minimum experience and training required
- Mental skill and knowledge
- Physical requirements
- Problem-solving skills
- Accountability

Everyone who fills this position will be paid exactly the same; in other words, the job has a certain salary value, and anyone occupying that position draws that salary. A lot of schools base their teachers' salaries on the Job Worth system.

If a Market Worth system is used, the salary will be commensurate with what the competition (the market) is paying, based on industry standards. Small- to medium-sized companies generally use this system. The market, and therefore the salary, will differ in various geographical areas, because the cost to live in cities such as New York City and Los Angeles is more than to live in, say, a small town in central Kansas.

The company's ability to pay is, of course, also a crucial factor in salary determination. Small and brand-new companies may not have the revenue of larger, more established companies so they might offer non-monetary benefits instead of higher salaries. These benefits could vary from a free parking space to days off to flextime scheduling.

The company may use your last or current salary as a factor in their offer, but it is not always a fair judge of how much you're worth. You may have added educational and skill levels that were not required in that job.

Demand (as in market demand) is another possible factor. If the demand is high, meaning that there are too few qualified applicants to fill available positions, employers are more likely to offer higher salaries. The opposite may be true when the market is saturated with applicants.

You're probably wondering what to do with all this information. How is this going to help you with negotiating when you receive an offer? Now that you know the factors that determine salary, you can personalize your package for negotiation. To do this, you need information on the range of salaries in your geographical area, the skills required for the position, the market demand, and the "scoop" on the company. Guess what? You are going to do more research. Where? The Internet offers a wealth of information, and here are also some places where you can obtain salary surveys that contain comparative information on average wages across different occupations, regions of the country, and levels of experience:

- Annual State Occupational Guides.
- Publications such as your local newspapers and news and trade magazines. *U.S. News & World Report* is an excellent source as they conduct annual surveys and publish valuable information on companies and job availability.
- College placement offices.
- Peers and people you know who are in the field.
- *Are You Paid What You're Worth?* by Michael O'Malley, Broadway Books, New York.
- Recruiters and headhunters.

The Internet offers salary surveys at the following websites:

- www.careers.wsj.com   Wall Street Journal-link to WSJ Jobs
- www.bls.gov   Link to BLS Jobs
- http://hotjobs.yahoo.com   Link to Yahoo Jobs
- www.yahoo.com/culture/organizations/professional
- www.yahoo.com/business   Link to Yahoo Business News
- www.yahoo.com/economy/organizations/trade associations
- www.salary.com   Link to Salary Guide-Monster with www.Monster.com (good location)
- www.wageweb.com   Data on benefits, pay practices, 39 different jobs. Key in comp.datasurvey.com/
- www.newslink.org

When you know the salary ranges for your area, the skills required, the market demand, and have the "scoop" on the company that has made you an offer, you're ready to assess your market value: what *you* are worth. Complete the forms on the next three pages and use them as a guide to help you determine the wage you can ask for.

Negotiating Your Benefits

Your compensation package includes benefits as well as salary. These, too, can be negotiated, so you should be prepared and not always accept what is offered if the benefits do not meet your needs. When deciding whether to reject or accept an offer, remember that money isn't everything, and that you can sometimes actually make *more* money with things like bonuses and stock options—anywhere from 30 to 60 percent of your base salary—than by receiving a higher salary. Some benefits, such as Social Security, unemployment, and workers' compensation, are mandated (all employers must offer them by law) and some are voluntary. Employers are

DETERMINING YOUR PRICE TAG

Position Being Considered: _____

What are the skills and qualifications for this position? _____

_____

_____

_____

_____

_____

_____

_____

_____

What did I find is the average salary for this type of job? _____

What are my skills and qualifications as compared to the average worker in this position? _____

_____

_____

_____

_____

_____

_____

_____

_____

_____

_____

_____

Based on the information above, I believe that I am worth $ _____ in annual (monthly, hourly) salary; therefore, I will request wages in the range of $ _____ to $ _____ .

YOUR BOTTOM LINE

What do you think you are worth? What is the job worth?

In Chapter 1, you evaluated the things that you value. Now is the time to determine if the job really offers the things you value—or the salary level you require. In the Interests, Wants, and Needs area in Chapter 1 you answered some questions titled "What Do I Want?" You can now evaluate the job offer to see if the job offer provides those things.

YOUR BOTTOM LINE _____

SALARY

_____ Hourly Wage

_____ Monthly Salary

_____ Annual Salary

QUALITY OF WORK LIFE

_____ Respect

_____ Scope of Responsibilities

_____ Professional Environment

_____ Coworker Compatibility

_____ Management Compatibility

_____ Advancement Opportunity or Career Path

_____ Time Off (Leisure Time)

_____

_____

_____

_____

_____

_____

BENEFITS

_____ Full Medical—Employer Paid

_____ Full Medical—with Copay

_____ Family Medical—Employer Paid

_____ Family Medical—with Copay

_____ Dental

_____ Vision

_____ Prescriptions

_____ Uniform Allowance

_____ Travel Allowance

_____ Cafeteria Plan

_____ Life Insurance

_____ Disability Insurance

_____ Pay for Time Not Worked/Overtime

_____ Retirement Plan

_____ Tuition Reimbursement

_____ Higher Salary if Some Benefits Waived

_____

_____

_____

_____

YOUR NEGOTIATING LINE

What will make you very happy? (Realistically)

Negotiating Line _____!

SALARY

_____   Hourly Wage

_____   Monthly Salary

_____   Annual Salary

QUALITY OF WORK LIFE

_____

_____

_____

_____

_____

_____

_____

_____

_____

_____

BENEFITS

_____

_____

_____

_____

_____

_____

_____

_____

_____

_____

realizing that in this day and age, they must change their thinking about what constitutes a benefits package. According to James E. Challenger, "Companies are offering 'soft benefits' that are designed to give employees more time to work and enjoy life."[1] Employees now enjoy perks such as car washes at lunch and in-house dry cleaning. Some companies even adjust work schedules to allow early quitting times on Fridays during the summer. Other benefits that could be offered are relocation assistance, vacation time, stock options, club memberships, commissions, or even company cars. So before you negotiate with an employer for a benefit package, be aware of what you need and what is available to you. As you can see, there is no standard list of perks. The typical employee benefit package includes 10 annual paid holidays and 9.4 vacation days after a year of service. About 75 percent of companies offer some kind of health insurance, and now more employers are asking for larger contributions from their employees toward the cost of the plan.[2] What you have to do is to evaluate each of the perks and decide which will benefit you. After you have done your research and have a good idea of what you want in benefits, use the Benefit Checklist on pages 152 and 153. Your objective is to negotiate the maximum benefit package possible. Keep in mind that, based on the current economics of the country, benefits can cost the employer anywhere from 15 to 40+ percent of your salary, so it is in the company's best interest to keep those costs to minimum. This is the reason they require employees to contribute a larger share of the cost.

Negotiating the Offer

Once you've established your worth and have the compensation package that you believe you deserve firmly in mind, the next step is negotiating with the employer. This step requires that you know what benefits you can bring to the company and are prepared to sell them. Why should an employer agree to give you the compensation for which you are asking? What are *you* offering in return? Why are you worth the figure you're asking? This is another time when your Job Skills Portfolio will assist you in selling your value to the employer. If you've done your research, you will know what the company's needs are and how you can help to fill those needs. Your job is to convince *them* you can fill their needs. Assure the employer that you are as interested in meeting the company's goals as well as your own. Keep your negotiation focused, and don't get sidetracked into talking only about your needs. You are paid a salary, not because you need a new computer, car, or house or because your kid needs braces, but because of your worth to the company. Do not under any circumstances let the negotiation become an adversarial (me against you) relationship by becoming argumentative or emotional. Your objective should be a win/win solution.

Negotiating Tips

Ask for what you want (and negotiate if your request is declined)

If you don't ask, you may never get what you want, and more likely, you will get your bottom line (or lower). Be comfortable with silence. The person with the least tolerance of silence will attempt to fill the void by speaking—many times by offering to compromise.

If the proposed salary is too low, try to negotiate other ways to achieve both your goals and those of the prospective employer

Be flexible: Introduce ways besides salary that will achieve both your goals and those of the prospective employer. You might want to negotiate the benefit package. For example, if you don't need the medical insurance and it costs the company $200 per month, decline coverage and ask for half of the premium to be added to your salary—a $100 increase for you and a $100 savings for the company. You might propose that the employer enlarge the job to give you more latitude in salary range. If you are going to do more than the current job description, a higher salary is appropriate.

Don't let the employer negotiate your salary down with non-monetary perks

Accept this only if the perks are ones that you place a high value on and would be happy with.

Avoid providing a specific salary figure, if possible, until the full negotiation of the position and other factors have been resolved

Don't be the first to give a definitive figure; ask for the salary range of that position. If pressed, say that you believe your qualifications probably place you somewhere between the midpoint and maximum salary range and resell your best features again at this time. Understanding that there is a "going rate" range for similar personnel in the workforce and knowing what that range is lets you state a figure at the midpoint or higher level.

If asked, discuss your current salary honestly

Sometime during the negotiating process, you may be asked a question about your current or most recent salary. How you answer this question could be a strong deciding factor in the salary offered you by the interviewer. Be truthful when you give them a figure, of course, and be sure to include your non-monetary compensation in addition to your base salary.

Know the benefits available in the workplace

For example, some companies offer ten paid holidays a year, and others may offer more. Some offer one week of vacation with pay after one year, others may offer two weeks after a year. Some offer only a maximum of two weeks of vacation no matter how long you work for the company, while others allow you to take additional weeks of paid vacation per year after a certain number of years of employment. Not all health plans cover what you need. For example, some require you to use the plan's doctors, others allow you to use the plan's doctors at one rate (plan pays 100 percent) or to use doctors outside the plan at another rate (60/40—the plan pays 60 percent, you pay 40 percent). Keep in mind the benefits you want, including what kind of flexibility you want in a medical plan.

Be sure to check out websites on the Internet by simply keying in "Employee Benefits." If you aren't sure how to use the websites, go to your local library and research information on individual employee benefits. While you're there, also check out Michael O'Malley's book, *Are You Paid What You're Worth?*, for some excellent tips on negotiating salaries, benefits, bonuses, and salary raises.

Negotiate from a position of strength and with enthusiasm

How do you do this? Simple: Sell the employer on the idea that you are the best solution to the company's problems. If the employer has offered you the job, she has made the decision that you are the number one choice. Having selected you as number one, the employer will negotiate, to a point, to hire you rather than settle for their second or third choice. This gives you an advantage and a strong negotiating position. If you express your enthusiasm for the position and resell your abilities to meet the employer's needs, you will indeed be negotiating from a position of some power.

Have your completed Bottom Line and Negotiating Line checklists available when negotiating

With this information readily available to you, you can usually make an immediate decision to accept the position or not. If you are not completely sure, the alternative is to say "I very much appreciate this offer; I believe it is an exciting opportunity for me, and I would like to think it over. If it's acceptable to you, may I call you tomorrow with my answer?" If the offer is too low, you can renegotiate by saying something such as "I am really thrilled with your offer and am highly motivated to work for your company; I know I can do an excellent job for you. However, based on my research of salary ranges for comparable positions, I believe my qualifications warrant a higher salary. Would it be possible to meet again and take another look at the salary to see if we can somehow reach a position where I could help you meet your needs and, at the same time, be given the salary commensurate with my qualifications?"

Be gracious

Allow the employer to feel that he or she has won some compromises. "You've got to live with these people after you join them," says Scott Kingdom, managing director of the Chicago office of Korn/Ferry, the nation's biggest headhunting firm.[3]

Additional Considerations

In addition to the salary and benefits, a few other things warrant your attention. Are the company itself, the physical environment, and the personnel what you are looking for in a job?

- *The company:* Is it large or small, new to the community or an older, respected and reliable organization? Is the company progressive? Is the industry that it's in expanding or receding? Does the company have a policy manual (or written statements) regarding its policies on employee vacations, terminations, and working conditions?

- *The physical environment:* Where is the company located? Is it in a "better" part of town or in an inconvenient or even dangerous area? What do the buildings, furnishings, and equipment reflect: pride or indifference? Where will you be working: in the back of the building away from everyone, or up front where the action is? Where would you like to be?

- *The people:* What kind of people work for this company? Are they primarily of one age group, and is it yours? Who is going to be your immediate supervisor? Have you met this person and does your intuition tell you you could work comfortably with him or her? In your interactions with this company during pre-interview and interview visits, how were you treated? Were you made to feel at ease and welcome? How did the employees interact with each other? How would you describe the company and the people, and will you be happy and productive working with these people?

- *The job:* How is this job going to affect your personal life? Is it going to require that you be away from home frequently, possibly on weekends, limiting your time with your family and friends? Do you know exactly what you will be doing during the day? Where does this position lead? What are your chances for promotion, transferring to other departments, and learning new skills?

Make the decision to accept or not accept a job offer based on all of the forgoing items. This decision is a vital one that will affect your life, your happiness, and your well-being. You should not make it hastily without carefully considering all the ramifications. If you've prepared an error-free resume and cover letter,

EMPLOYEE BENEFIT CHECKLIST

○ Health Plan

_____ Employee Only—Company Paid

_____ Copay Premium for Employee

_____ Family

_____ Type _____ PPO _____ HMO _____ Other

_____ Dental

_____ Vision

_____ Rx Plan

_____ Wellness (Physical Exams)

○ Life Insurance

_____ Times _____ Year's Salary

_____ Additional Coverage Available

○ Disability Income Plan

○ Dependent Card—Child Care Assistance

○ Employee Assistance Programs (EAPs)

○ Payment for Time Not Worked/Overtime

_____ Vacation Policy

_____ Paid Holidays

_____ Comp Time

_____ Overtime Compensation

_____ Personal Leave of Absence (w/o pay)

_____ Funeral Leave

_____ Jury Duty

_____ Military Leave

_____ Inclement Weather Absences (office closed down)

_____ Sick Leave

○ Retirement Plans

_____ Profit Sharing Plans

_____ 401(k) Plans

_____ SEP (Simplified Employee Pension)

(continued)

EMPLOYEE BENEFIT CHECKLIST Continued

_____ Keogh Plans

_____ Employee Stock Option Plans (ESOPs)

○ Pay Raises _____ Annual _____ Other _____ Merit _____ Negotiated

○ Cafeteria Plan

_____ Pretax Savings of Medical Premiums/Child Care/Adult Care

○ Pay Status

_____ Exempt Only basis for exemption from being paid overtime is if you are classified as:

_____ Executive (managers)

_____ Administrative (for those who carry out the policies of the company)

_____ Outside Sales

_____ Computer Related (primarily programmers and systems analysts)

_____ Professional (requires advanced degrees—teachers, lawyers, artistic endeavors)

○ Pay Periods

_____ Monthly

_____ Biweekly

_____ Twice a Month

○ Salary/Wages

$_____ Hourly

$_____ Biweekly/Twice a Month

$_____ Monthly

$_____ Annually

○ Travel

_____ If you have to travel on behalf of your employer, are you compensated for using your car? (approximately _____ cents per mile)

○ Tuition Assistance (for job-related courses)

○ Other Benefits

_____

_____

_____

have studied the tips on how to interview effectively, and have matched the job to your personal assessment of values and needs, you are well on your way to getting your ideal job with an ideal compensation package. The bottom line is, only *you* can decide whether or not the job is right for you.

Keeping the Job

The business world is a totally different world than the one you've been used to in college. The principles and norms you have followed throughout grade school, high school, and college don't really apply to the business world. You could encounter office politics and may have to get used to being scrutinized in a different way. Once you have your job, do you know how to *keep* that job and acquire a promotion, a raise? Can you convince your employer that he/she made the right decision? Your previous experience and job history are now less important than your ability to prove that you can do the job for which you were hired. What are the major priorities that employers have for all employees, and what are the things which can cause you to get a dreaded "pink slip"? What happens if there is a recession and your company has to reorganize and lay off some of their employees? Suppose your company decides to outsource some jobs to other countries? No job is fail-proof. You should be aware of these factors which can influence whether you keep and/or progress in your new job. It's wise to plan how you would deal with any of the above factors to avoid being laid off, let go, outsourced, and so on.

To avoid being outsourced or laid off, you must have or acquire the skills and education levels that are above the jobs being outsourced that anyone can do. Jobs such as those in manufacturing have all but disappeared because there is very little training required to do these. Also, because a back-office job that nets $100 an hour here in the states only gets $20 an hour in India, guess where these jobs are going. An aerospace engineer in Russia: $600 a month; in the U.S: $3000. It's estimated that by 2015, 3.3 million white-collar jobs and $136 billion in wages will shift from the U.S. to low-cost countries.[4] This is very important if you want to stay ahead of the game and keep your job. Skilled workers are at such a premium that employers are offering training to employees whom they want to keep. These guidelines also pertain to employees of companies that are downsizing and reorganizing. Employers are not going to eliminate workers who have or are willing to obtain the skills and education that help to make the company more profit. Another protection against being outsourced is to become fluent in another language. If you are an English-speaking person, two other languages that are very much in demand are Spanish and an oriental language.

Aside from the factors mentioned above that are present in the workplace, there are other things that are viewed by employers on a day-to-day basis as reasons to place you on probation or to dismiss you. Three of the major expectations of employers are appearance, skills, and work behavior.

Appearance

Employers view you as an extension of their company; therefore, how you look is critical to your keeping your job, especially if you are in a position where you are meeting with the public or customers. Your attire and grooming and hygiene are two factors of your overall appearance which will be judged by

CLOSING THE JOB SEARCH PROCESS   **155**

employers. Are you clean, neat, and wearing clothes that are not too baggy or tight? Are your clothes appropriate for your age, your position in the company? Is your perfume or aftershave so strong that your boss smells you before he/she sees you? Do you appear to be going out to the cocktail lounge for happy hour? Remember, this is the workplace, not a party. If you have doubts about what is expected, ask for some feedback and criticisms from your immediate supervisor or employer. Go back and reread the suggestions in Chapter 4 on professional dress which are pertinent not just to getting the job, but also to keeping it. Appearance is definitely a vital factor in the consideration of who is awarded promotions. You've probably heard the saying, "Clothes make the person." If you doubt that, think how often we judge others by the way they dress.

Skills

In every job, there are always extra skills you can acquire to better perform your job and also to be eligible for promotions. Do you have related experience that would enhance your ability to perform the job? Are you willing to learn new skills, take classes to upgrade your performance? Are you willing to take advice from others above you that can give you feedback about the manner in which you do your job? Try to learn from those above you, your supervisors and managers. Shadowing (paying close attention and observing others who are where you want to be) is an excellent practice to learn more about what is required for the position you want. Keep in mind that intangible, transferrable skills have universal appeal. Those abilities to collaborate, organize, persuade, listen, think critically, and manage your time are just a few that are valued by companies in most all fields and businesses. With respect to the position you hold and the company where you are now employed, consider which of the transferrable skills are the most valuable. Work on improving those you have and acquiring those you don't.

Work Behavior

Attendance, dependability, and reliability are characteristics of behavior that can influence whether or not you are going to keep your job and advance in it. Do you come to work regularly, on time and not late? Do you complete assignments and projects on time? Can you be counted upon to do the job correctly? Do you take more initiative rather than just doing what you can get by with? In other terms, are you reliable and dependable? Another aspect of work behavior which could get you fired is your personality. If you have a negative attitude, you are not polite, or you can't get along with your coworkers and supervisor, these are definitely behaviors which could get you that dreaded pink slip. For every one dismissal based on job performance, there are two to three that are given because of an employee's poor communication and not getting along with others. If you are having difficulty with these behaviors and you are otherwise a valued employee, you might be required to take a personality assessment test such as the Myers-Briggs or a Gallup test. These tests help the employer to determine what you would need to change in order to be a better team member and to improve on your people skills. The tests also assist employers in determining what kinds of job assignments fit your personality. If you are working in an environment not suitable to your personality, your production level goes down and your attitude creates problems for everyone. One thing to remember is that you have the power to choose your response to any circumstance in your work environment, so begin your work day with a positive attitude.

Some of the day-to-day "no-no's" that also could get you fired are using your company's computer for personal messages (many employers are now monitoring their employees' emails and Internet usage) and stealing your employer's pencils, paper, and work items such as tools, equipment, ideas, plans, and so on. Yes, it IS stealing, not borrowing nor is it "owed" to you! One behavior that is guaranteed to cause you trouble with your coworkers and supervisor is bringing your personal problems to work and discussing details of your personal life with your coworkers, bosses, and customers. A very risky behavior is airing your complaints with others on the job and company clients.

Positive Behaviors to Help You Keep the Job

Well, now that we've covered the behaviors that could get you fired, let's discuss some positives that help you to keep the job. A positive behavior that can get good points is to determine the priorities and goals of the company and find ways to help the company move toward them. Speak with your boss to discover what the priorities are, what your part can be to assist the company in realizing those goals, and brainstorm with her to set specific goals for you. Generally, the main two priorities of most companies are saving time and making money, except those of course who are non-profit companies. Therefore, a way that you can earn high marks is to show your employer that you can assist in this. This is excellent insurance against being eliminated. Keep in close contact with your immediate supervisor regarding your performance and find out about advancement opportunities. Monitor your progress in those goals, and then set new goals and acquire the necessary education and skills to acquire them. Be creative, think of a new idea that will improve the company's bottom line, sales, or services. Maybe you have a way for the company to cut costs, but you're just not sure about how to go about it. Engage your team members to help you; research shows that people working in groups are much more imaginative and creative than previously thought. Even if you're a factory worker, companies have found new ideas many times come from those employees "in the trenches."

The Right Way to Ask for a Raise

Another way to get pushed out the door toward the unemployment line is to inappropriately ask for more money. If you believe you deserve a higher salary and are going to ask your boss for a raise, there is a right way and a wrong way to do it.

The first and foremost thing you should do is to review the company policies regarding compensation. If it is written in the policy manual that raises are only awarded at certain intervals and for specific accomplishments, you must be aware of these before approaching your supervisor for a raise. Timing is very important! It is especially a good time after you've received an award or maybe saved money for your firm. Consider the status of the company budget; if sales and profits are down, there might not be enough money to grant raises. Also, try to arrange an appointment with your boss at a favorable non-busy time of the day and week. Here is a brief list of steps you should consider before speaking with your boss about a raise.

1. Do a salary survey to get the range of salaries being awarded for your kind of position. Have a clear idea of the salary you desire. If your present salary is below the average income, all other things being equal, you probably have a good chance of getting a raise.

2. Put together all documentation of your accomplishments which have been noted on your performance appraisals which you have in your portfolio to present to your superior as justification for your increase in salary. After you have put your documents together, rehearse! Practice your presentation aloud until it is polished and professional; this will also give you more confidence.

3. Do not, I repeat, *do not* attempt to find out the salaries of your coworkers as a measure of equality. If your employer finds out that you have done this, I can almost assure you that you will need to get your resume out and upgrade it. I have seen this happen in many companies where I and others I know have worked. Your raise will be granted, not because of the salaries of others, but because of your own merits. There are other avenues to pursue and acquire salary information. Go to the online salary sites such as the ones given on page 145. Other excellent sources are MSN Careers salary calculator, CBsalary.com, the Bureau of Labor Statistics, and industry websites.

4. In the meeting with your superior, you could get one of three reactions. She might say "No" or "No, I'll have to speak with my boss." Or, you might get a "Yes." If you're turned down for the raise you asked for, be prepared to negotiate. If she said that she has to speak with her supervisor, ask when you should get back to her. If it is a firm "no," you could suggest other means of compensation you would be willing to receive or ask if you can meet with her in a few months. Set a date at that time which is acceptable to her.

I sincerely hope this chapter has given you some assistance in knowing how to properly and successfully close your interviews, acquire a fair and equitable salary and benefit package, and how to keep the job you worked so hard to obtain. I wish you success in earning promotions and salary raises appropriate for you and your skills and abilities. Good luck in all your future endeavors.

NOTES

1. James E. Challenger, Job Decision Isn't Just About the Money, January 16, 2000.
2. Walker Information Global Network, 2000 Walker Information, Inc.
3. "How to Negotiate," *U.S. News & World Report*, November 1, 1999, 92. Copyright U.S. News & World Report, L.P. Reprinted by permission.
4. "Is Your Job Next?" *BusinessWeek*, February 3, 2003.

Appendix

Postal Service Guidelines

The U.S. Postal Service offers these guidelines to ensure that your mail gets delivered quickly and accurately:

Write or type envelopes in all capital letters using no commas.

Always use your return address.

Always put the attention line above the firm name.

Include in the delivery address line either the street address, the PO Box number, rural route number, or the highway contract route number.

Indicate whether or not it's N, S, E, or W.

Include the RM (room), STE (suite), or APT (apartment) number.

Reserve the last line solely for the city, state, and ZIP code.

Use the ZIP code, and if you know the ZIP + 4 code, use that.

STATE ABBREVIATIONS

Alabama AL	Louisiana LA	Ohio OH
Alaska AK	Maine ME	Oklahoma OK
Arizona AZ	Maryland MD	Oregon OR
Arkansas AR	Massachusetts MA	Pennsylvania PA
California CA	Michigan MI	Puerto Rico PR
Colorado CO	Minnesota MN	Rhode Island RI
Connecticut CT	Mississippi MS	South Carolina SC
Delaware DE	Missouri MO	South Dakota SD
District of Columbia DC	Montana MT	Tennessee TN
Florida FL	Nebraska NE	Texas TX
Georgia GA	Nevada NV	Utah UT
Hawaii HI	New Hampshire NH	Vermont VT
Idaho ID	New Jersey NJ	Virginia VA
Illinois IL	New Mexico NM	Washington WA
Indiana IN	New York NY	West Virginia WV
Iowa IA	North Carolina NC	Wisconsin WI
Kansas KS	North Dakota ND	Wyoming WY
Kentucky KY		

STANDARD ABBREVIATIONS

Avenue AVE	Expressway EXPY	Road RD
Boulevard BLVD	Freeway FWY	Square SQ
Circle CIR	Lane LN	Street ST
Court CT	Parkway PKY	Turnpike TPKE

Figuring Monthly Income and Expenses

Before you speak with an employer about a salary, you should be fully aware of how much it costs you to live each month. Most people have very little idea how much they spend each month or why they run out of money. Rather than having a budget plan for paying bills first and then paying for entertainment and non-necessities, people often do the reverse. To meet your financial obligations, you must know what your income and expenses are and budget accordingly.

Using the Income and Expense form provided, or one that you prefer, figure out the salary you need to be able to live comfortably and to pay your bills. In the section for nonfixed expenses, inflate your figures rather than using a minimum amount. Allow for more rather than fewer expenses, so that if you do incur extra expenses, you'll have the money to pay for them. If extra is left over at the end of the month, put it in your savings account or buy something you've been wanting. It's better to have a nice surprise at the end of the month rather than a rude awakening when you discover that you need to fix your car or buy school supplies for your child—and you've already spent the money. I design and teach budgeting classes at several colleges for students of all ages, and it never fails to amaze me at how very little the average person knows about how to stay within his or her income level. This is the main reason why applicants when given a salary figure don't realize that it is probably less than what they need to live on. If you've done your homework beforehand, you will know how much salary you need to be able to stay out of debt.

TIPS FOR MANAGING YOUR BUDGET

- *Keep track of everything you spend.* This is the area where most people get into trouble; they simply do not realize how much they're spending on trivial, unnecessary items. Ask for receipts for everything you buy. It is also the area over which you have the most control. If you keep track, you'll be able to see your spending trends honestly and where you can cut down if need be.

- *Set goals for extras.* If you want new clothes, DVDs, pleasure trips, and so on, plan their purchase. Look ahead to a bonus, commission, or tax refund and earmark the extra money for your purchases. Don't fool yourself into thinking you'll manage by working overtime, cutting down on food, or going without your fun money. You won't!

- *Save money through wise shopping, do-it-yourself projects, and finding free events for entertainment.* Check local libraries and community centers for free shows, musicals, workshops, and holiday events. When you see something you want, before buying it, stall. Walk around the store or mall for 20 minutes, get a cup of coffee, do anything that will give you time to think about it and to check your budget (which you should carry with you when you shop). Do you really need it? Can you afford it? Is it really a bargain? Learn how to do your own hair, change the oil in your car, upholster your frayed couch or chair, fix that broken door, etc.

- *Examine your thinking.* How you feel about money affects how and what you buy or save. Where do you want to be six months or a year from now? Develop a money consciousness. If you are not truly serious about changing your spending habits, paying your bills on time, and getting the things you know you deserve when you can afford them, all the tips in the world won't help you. If you are serious and committed to living responsibly, go to the next page and complete your Income and Expense sheet.

- *Make a list of your five biggest money problems.* State how you contributed to these five problems and brainstorm ways to solve them. You will probably discover that you are part of the problem.

Ⓜ ONTHLY INCOME AND EXPENSE FORM

MONTHLY INCOME

Wages, salary, tips $ _____

Alimony, child support   _____

Dividends from stocks, mutual funds, etc.   _____

Interest on savings accounts, bonds, CDs, etc.   _____

Social Security benefits   _____

Pensions   _____

Other income   _____

Total Monthly Income $ _____

FIXED EXPENSES

Savings $ _____

Rent/mortgage payment   _____

Utilities   _____

Telephone, Internet, cable, etc.   _____

Insurance (health, home, life, auto)   _____

Taxes (income, real estate)   _____

Installment payments (credit cards, car, department store accounts, etc.)   _____

Other installment loans (school, etc.)   _____

Subscriptions/memberships   _____

Medical (doctors, medicines, etc.)   _____

Child care   _____

Other   _____

Total Fixed Expenses $ _____

(continued)

Ⓜ ONTHLY INCOME AND EXPENSE FORM Continued

NONFIXED (FLUCTUATING) EXPENSES

Food $ _____

Household services/expenses   _____

Transportation/car maintenance   _____

Clothing   _____

Furnishings/equipment   _____

Personal care (grooming, cosmetics)   _____

Recreation/entertainment   _____

Gifts/contributions   _____

Other   _____

Total Nonfixed Expenses $ _____

Total Monthly Expenses $ _____

TOTAL MONTHLY DISCRETIONARY INCOME*

Total monthly income $ _____

Minus total monthly expenses   _____

Equals your NET CASH FLOW $ _____

*This amount reflects the amount of money you have available to put in savings or to spend on extras.

POST-INTERVIEW SELF-EVALUATION

1. Was I punctual, even early, for my interview? If not, why not?

   _____

   _____

   _____

   _____

2. Was my appearance appropriate and above reproach? Are there any areas that need improvement?

   _____

   _____

   _____

   _____

3. How would I rate my handshake?

   _____

   _____

   _____

   _____

4. What questions were asked of me that I feel I didn't answer adequately? How could I improve on them?

   _____

   _____

   _____

   _____

5. Was I relaxed, self-confident, and friendly?

   _____

6. Did I sell myself with marketable skills applicable to the job for which I was applying? If not, should I rewrite my marketing appraisal and examine my Job Skills Portfolio to determine if my skills listed are a match to the ones required by the companies to which I've applied?

   _____

   _____

   _____

   _____

(continued)

POST-INTERVIEW SELF-EVALUATION Continued

7. How would I rate my communication (oral and written) before and during the interview? If it needs improvement, how am I going to correct this?

_____

_____

_____

_____

8. What kind of body language did I convey to the interviewer? Was it open and friendly?

_____

_____

_____

_____

9. Were there things I forgot to tell the interviewer or to ask the interviewer? (Include them in your thank-you letter or follow-up call.)

_____

_____

_____

_____

_____

_____

_____

_____

_____

10. Am I scheduled for a second interview? (If so, write the date, time, location, and the name of the interviewer.)

_____

_____

_____

_____

ATTIRE/GROOMING TIPS

FOR MEN

1. Wear a long-sleeved shirt.

2. Make sure your tie is one within the current fashion. Don't wear a tie with funny sayings or cutesy pictures on it, or a bow tie. Best choices are solid colors, polka dots, foulard, or paisley. Patterned ties should be worn with solid-colored shirts.

3. Tuck in your shirttail and make sure your tie is not showing below the back of your collar.

4. Don't have things bulging in your pockets or keys dangling from a chain on your belt.

5. Don't wear a pocket handkerchief.

6. Do wear a belt in either brown, cordovan, or black, definitely coordinated with your clothes colors.

7. If you wear an overcoat or hat, leave it in the outer office.

8. If you have facial hair, have it cut in an acceptable style. Make sure it is well trimmed and groomed.

9. Wear a watch.

10. Coordinate the colors of your suit, tie, shirt, socks, and shoes.

11. Beware of using too much aftershave, but do be certain you have good personal hygiene.

FOR WOMEN

1. Choose a hairstyle that will convey moderation and confidence; it should be modern and stylish.

2. If you carry a briefcase, don't carry a purse. If you carry a purse, clean it out before the interview.

3. Always wear a slip and be sure that it comes to above your skirt hemline.

4. Don't wear open-toed sandals or very high-heeled shoes.

5. Wear a skirt or dress with the hemline at or below the knees, even if the current rage is short skirts.

6. Always wear stockings, and they must be run-free. Bring an extra pair in case of an accident.

7. Don't wear pants: Even though they may be acceptable for work, it's risky to wear them to an interview. You may disagree with this, but research shows that women are viewed more favorably when dressed in a skirt or dress. Obviously, this will be contingent upon what field you're in and where you will be working.

8. Wear a watch.

9. Don't wear any flirtatious or overly feminine clothes and choose accessories that accentuate your clothing.

10. Check the heels of your shoes for scuff marks, and polish them if necessary.

11. Don't overdo fragrances (perfume), but make certain you have good personal hygiene.

HOW TO TIE A TIE

THE WINDSOR KNOT

Wide and triangular—for widespread shirt collar

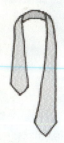

1 Start with wide end of tie on your right and extending a foot below narrow end.

2 Cross wide end over narrow and bring up through loop.

3 Bring wide end down, around behind narrow, and up on your right.

4 Then put down through loop and around across narrow as shown.

5 Turn and pass up through loop and . . .

6 Complete by slipping down through the knot in front. Tighten and draw up snug to collar.

THE FOUR-IN-HAND KNOT

Long and straight—to complement a standard shirt collar

1 Start with wide end of tie on your right and extending a foot below narrow end.

2 Cross wide end over narrow, and back underneath.

3 Continue around, passing wide end across front of narrow once more.

4 Pass wide end up through loop.

5 Holding front of knot loose with index finger, pass wide end down through loop in front.

6 Remove finger and tighten knot carefully. Draw up tight to collar by holding narrow end and sliding knot up snug.

(continued)

HOW TO TIE A TIE Continued

THE HALF-WINDSOR KNOT

Medium symmetrical triangle—for standard shirt collars

 1 Start with wide end of tie on your right and extending a foot below narrow end.

 2 Cross wide end over narrow part and turn back underneath.

 3 Bring up and turn down through loop.

 4 Pass wide end around front from left to right.

 5 Then, up through loop.

 6 And down through knot in front. Tighten carefully and draw up to collar.

THE BOW TIE

Long and straight—to complement a standard shirt collar, but not recommended for interviews

 1 Start with end in left hand extending 1-1/2" below that in right hand.

 2 Cross longer end over shorter end and pass up through loop.

 3 Form front loop of bow by doubling up shorter end (hanging) and placing across collar points.

 4 Hold this front loop with thumb and forefinger of left hand. Drop long end down over front.

 5 Place right forefinger, pointing up, on bottom half of hanging part. Pass up behind front loop and . . .

 6 Push resulting loop through knot behind front loop (see illustration). Even ends and tighten.

U.S. Department of Justice
Immigration and Naturalization Service

OMB No. 1115-0136
Employment Eligibility Verification

Please read instructions carefully before completing this form. The instructions must be available during completion of this form. ANTI-DISCRIMINATION NOTICE. It is illegal to discriminate against work eligible individuals. Employers CANNOT specify which document(s) they will accept from an employee. The refusal to hire an individual because of a future expiration date may also constitute illegal discrimination.

Section 1. Employee Information and Verification. To be completed and signed by employee at the time employment begins

Print Name: Last	First	Middle Initial	Maiden Name

Address (Street Name and Number)	Apt. #	Date of Birth (month/day/year)

City	State	Zip Code	Social Security #

I am aware that federal law provides for imprisonment and/or fines for false statements or use of false documents in connection with the completion of this form.

I attest, under penalty of perjury, that I am (check one of the following):
☐ A citizen or national of the United States
☐ A Lawful Permanent Resident (Alien # A _____)
☐ An alien authorized to work until _____ / _____ / _____
(Alien # or Admission # _____)

Employee's Signature	Date (month/day/year)

Preparer and/or Translator Certification. *(To be completed and signed if Section 1 is prepared by a person other than the employee.) I attest, under penalty of perjury, that I have assisted in the completion of this form and that to the best of my knowledge the information is true and correct.*

Preparer's/Translator's Signature	Print Name

Address (Street Name and Number, City, State, Zip Code)	Date (month/day/year)

Section 2. Employer Review and Verification. To be completed and signed by employer. Examine one document from list A OR examine one document from List B and one from List C as listed on the reverse of this form and record the title, number and expiration date, if any, of the document(s).

	List A	OR	List B	AND	List C
Document title:	_____		_____		_____
Issuing authority:	_____		_____		_____
Document #:	_____		_____		_____
Expiration Date (if any):	__ / __ / __		__ / __ / __		__ / __ / __
Document #:	_____				
Expiration Date (if any):	__ / __ / __				

CERTIFICATION—I attest, under penalty of perjury, that I have examined the document(s) presented by the above-named employee, that the above-listed document(s) appear to be genuine and to relate to the employee named, that the employee began employment on *(month/day/year)* ____ / ____ / ____ **and that to the best of my knowledge the employee is eligible to work in the United States. (State employment agencies may omit the date the employee began employment).**

Signature of Employer or Authorized Representative	Print Name	Title

Business or Organization Name Address (Street Name and Number, City, State, Zip Code)	Date (month/day/year)

Section 3. Updating and Reverification. To be completed and signed by employer

A. New Name (if applicable)	B. Date of rehire (month/day/year) (if applicable)

C. If employee's previous grant of work authorization has expired, provide the information below for the document that establishes current employment eligibility.

Document Title: _____ Document #: _____ Expiration Date (if any): ____ / ____ / ____

I attest, under penalty of perjury, that to the best of my knowledge, this employee is eligible to work in the United States, and if the employee presented document(s), the document(s) I have examined appear to be genuine and to relate to the individual.

Signature of Employer or Authorized Representative	Date (month/day/year)

Form I-9 (Rev. 11-21-91) N

All employers are required by the U.S. Department of Justice's Immigration and Naturalization Service to verify their employees' eligibility for employment by having the employees complete an I-9 form. If the employers do not submit this information within two weeks after the hire date, they can be fined a substantial amount of money. If you are working in the United States on a green card, work visa, or under any special circumstance, you need to be prepared to submit the necessary documents to prove your eligibility.

U.S. Department of Justice
Immigration and Naturalization Service

OMB No. 1115-0136

Employment Eligibility Verification

INSTRUCTIONS
PLEASE READ ALL INSTRUCTIONS CAREFULLY BEFORE COMPLETING THIS FORM

Anti-Discrimination Notice. It is illegal to discriminate against any individual (other than an alien not authorized to work in the U.S.) in hiring, discharging, or recruiting or referring for a fee because of that individual's national origin or citizenship status. It is illegal to discriminate against work eligible individuals. Employers **CANNOT** specify which document(s) they will accept from an employee. The refusal to hire an individual because of a future expiration date may also constitute illegal discrimination.

Section 1—Employee. All employees, citizens and noncitizens, hired after November 6, 1986, must complete Section 1 of this form at the time of hire, which is the actual beginning of employment. **The employer is responsible for ensuring that Section 1 is timely and properly completed.**

Preparer/Translator Certification. The Preparer/Translator Certification must be completed if Section 1 is prepared by a person other than the employee. A preparer/translator may be used only when the employee is unable to complete Section 1 on his/her own. However, the employee must still sign Section 1 personally.

Section 2—Employer. For the purpose of completing this form, the term "employer" includes those recruiters and referrers for a fee who are agricultural associations, agricultural employers, or farm labor contractors.

Employers must complete Section 2 by examining evidence of identity and employment eligibility with three (3) business days of the date employment begins. If employees are authorized to work, but are unable to present the required document(s) with three business days, they must present a receipt for the application of the document(s) within three business days and the actual document(s) within ninety (90) days. However, if employers hire individuals for a duration of less than three business days, Section 2 must be completed at the time employment begins. **Employers must record:** 1) document title; 2) issuing authority; 3) document number; 4) expiration date, if any; and 5) the date employment begins. Employers must sign and date the certification. Employees must present original documents. Employers may, but are not required to, photocopy the document(s) presented. These photocopies may only be used for the verification process and must be retained with the I-9. **However, employers are still responsible for completing the I-9.**

Section 3—Updating and Reverification. Employers must complete Section 3 when updating and/or reverifying the I-9. Employers must reverify employment eligibility of their employees on or before the expiration date recorded in Section 1. Employers **CANNOT** specify which document(s) they will accept from an employee.

- If an employee's name has changed at the time this form is being updated/reverified, complete Block A.

- If an employee is rehired within three (3) years of the date this form was originally completed and the employee is still to be employed on the same basis as previously indicated on this form (updating), complete Block B and the signature block.

- If an employee is rehired within three (3) years of the date this form was originally completed and the employee's work authorization has expired or if a current employee's work authorization is about to expire (reverification), complete Block B and:
  - examine any document that reflects that the employee is authorized to work in the U.S. (see List A or C),
  - record the document title, document number and expiration date (if any) in Block C, and
  - complete the signature block.

Photocopying and Retaining Form I-9. A blank I-9 may be reproduced provided both sides are copied. The instructions must be available to all employees completing this form. Employers must retain completed I-9s for three (3) years after the date of hire or one (1) year after the date employment ends, whichever is later.

For more detailed information, you may refer to the INS Handbook for Employers, (Form M-274). You may obtain the handbook at your local INS office.

Privacy Act Notice. The authority for collecting this information is the Immigration Reform and Control Act of 1986, Pub. L. 99-603 (8 U.S.C. 1324a).

This information is for employers to verify the eligibility of individuals for employment to preclude the unlawful hiring, or recruiting or referring for a fee, of aliens who are not authorized to work in the United States.

This information will be used by employers as a record of their basis for determining eligibility of an employee to work in the United States. The form will be kept by the employer and made available for inspection by officials of the U.S. Immigration and Naturalization Service, the Department of Labor, and the Office of Special Counsel for Immigration Related Unfair Employment Practices.

Submission of the information required in this form is voluntary. However, an individual may not begin employment unless this form is completed since employers are subject to civil or criminal penalties if they do not comply with the Immigration Reform and Control Act of 1986.

Reporting Burden. We try to create forms and instructions that are accurate, can be easily understood, and which impose the least possible burden on you to provide us with information. Often this is difficult because some immigration laws are very complex. Accordingly, the reporting burden for this collection of information is computed as follows: 1) learning about this form, 5 minutes; 2) completing the form, 5 minutes; and 3) assembling and filing (recordkeeping) the form, 5 minutes, for an average of 15 minutes per response. If you have comments regarding the accuracy of this burden estimate, or suggestions for making this form simpler, you can write to both the Immigration and Naturalization Service, 425 I Street, N.W., Room 5304, Washington, D.C. 20538; and the Office of Management and Budget, Paperwork Reduction Project, OMB No. 1115-0136, Washington, D.C. 20503.

EMPLOYERS MUST RETAIN COMPLETED I-9
PLEASE DO NOT MAIL COMPLETED I-9 TO INS

LISTS OF ACCEPTABLE DOCUMENTS

LIST A		LIST B		LIST C
Documents that Establish Both Identity and Employment Eligibility	**OR**	**Documents that Establish Identity**	**AND**	**Documents that Establish Employment Eligibility**

LIST A — Documents that Establish Both Identity and Employment Eligibility

1. U.S. Passport (unexpired or expired)

2. Certificate of U.S. Citizenship (INS Form N-560 or N-561)

3. Certificate of Naturalization (INS Form N-550 or N-570)

4. Unexpired foreign passport, with I-551 stamp or attached INS Form I-94 indicating unexpired employment authorization

5. Alien Registration Receipt Card with photograph (INS Form I-151 or I-551)

6. Unexpired Temporary Resident Card (INS Form I-688)

7. Unexpired Employment Authorization Card (INS Form I-688A)

8. Unexpired Reentry Permit (INS Form I-327)

9. Unexpired Refugee Travel Document (INS Form I-571)

10. Unexpired Employment Authorization Document issued by the INS which contains a photography (INS Form I-688B)

LIST B — Documents that Establish Identity

1. Driver's license or ID card issued by a state or outlying possession of the United States provided it contains a photograph or information such as name, date of birth, sex, height, eye color, and address

2. ID card issued by federal, state, or local government agencies or entities provided it contains a photograph or information such as name, date of birth, sex, height, eye color, and address

3. School ID card with a photograph

4. Voter's registration card

5. U.S. Military card or draft record

6. Military dependent's ID card

7. U.S. Coast Guard Merchant Mariner Card

8. Native American tribal document

9. Driver's license issued by a Canadian government authority

For persons under age 18 who are unable to present a document listed above:

10. School record or report card

11. Clinic, doctor, or hospital record

12. Day-care or nursery school record

LIST C — Documents that Establish Employment Eligibility

1. U.S. social security card issued by the Social Security Administration (other than a card stating it is not valid for employment)

2. Certification of Birth Abroad issued by the Department of State (Form FS-545 or Form DS-1350)

3. Original or certified copy of a birth certificate issued by a state, county, municipal authority or outlying possession of the United States bearing an official seal

4. Native American tribal document

5. U.S. Citizen ID Card (INS Form I-197)

6. ID Card for use of Resident Citizen in the United States (INS Form I-179)

7. Unexpired employment authorization document issued by the INS (other than those listed under List A)

Illustrations of many of these documents appear in Part 8 of the Handbook for Employers (M-274)

Form I-9 (Rev. 11-21-91) N

JOHN E. JONES

11567 East 17th Street, Spokane, WA 01435
(509) 555-4587 (Please leave message)
johnjones95@aol.com

SUMMARY OF QUALIFICATIONS

Eight years' experience as a Surveyor. Proficiency, knowledge, and strengths in the
following areas: Surveying, Field Engineering, Mapping, Drafting, Blueprinting,
Supervision, Training, Customer Relations. Roads/Bridges: Commercial & Residential.

SUMMARY OF EXPERIENCE

Currently work as an independent contractor doing surveying and drafting for some firms
in the Spokane area. Contracts include boundaries, commercial, heavy construction, and
topographic jobs.

2003–2008   **Avery Structures, Inc.,** Spokane, WA
             Party Chief on large construction jobs. Responsible for surveying and
             drafting.

2000–2003   **Centennial Engineering,** Seattle, WA
             Party Chief for survey team in the construction of bridges and roads.
             Responsible for calculations and drafting on all phases of the jobs.

1998–2000   **J.R. Developers,** Tacoma, WA
             Party Chief completing all survey work on the subdivisions.

1994–1998   **Al Messahaq/Aramco,** Saudi Arabia
             Party Chief on all project work in Geodetic Control, roads and highways,
             in addition to plant layout.

EDUCATION

ITT Technical Institute, Spokane, Washington, 2003
2000 Hours in Map Drafting

Spokane School of Surveying & Mapping, Seattle, Washington, 2000
Certificate for 1600-hour program in Surveying and Mapping.

REFERENCES

Will be provided upon request.

JOHN E. JONES

11567 East 17th Street, Spokane, WA 01435
(509) 555-4587 (Please leave message)
johnjones95@aol.com

OBJECTIVE

A position in Computer Operations with progressively expanding responsibilities leading to an appointment to Systems Analyst

EDUCATION

Spokane Technical Institute, Spokane, Washington
672-hour course in Computer Programming & Operations. State Certified. Graduated with honors. GPA: 3.67

Washington State University, Seattle, Washington
Completed 15 semester hours in Computer Science, including mastering Fortran.

Seattle School of Surveying & Mapping, Seattle, Washington
Certificate, 1600-hour program in Surveying & Mapping.

ITT Technical Institute, Spokane, Washington
Map Drafting (2000 hours).

PROFESSIONAL EXPERIENCE

Computer Computations/Data Processing
Involved in all aspects of data retrieval from computations to design to the finished product in the land surveying industry.

Mathematical
Performed daily algebraic and trigonometric calculations.

Teamwork
Worked cooperatively and effectively in fast-paced, demanding environment with all members of surveying crew, and interacted with various executive key personnel.

EMPLOYMENT HISTORY

Party Chief position for the following companies:

- Avery Structures, Inc., Spokane, Washington
- Centennial Engineering, Seattle, Washington
- J.R. Developers, Tacoma, Washington
- Al Messahaq/ARAMCO, Saudi Arabia

JOHN E. JONES

11567 East 17th Street, Spokane, WA 01435
(509) 555-4587 (Please leave message)
johnjones95@aol.com

OBJECTIVE

A position in Data Processing, preferably in Computer Operations or Programming. Five-Year Career Goal: Systems Analysis Management

SUMMARY OF QUALIFICATIONS

COMPUTER SCIENCE, OPERATIONS & PROGRAMMING—Two years Computer Programming with emphasis in the following languages, software and operating systems: BASIC, FORTRAN, COBOL, MS-DOS, EXCEL, DBASE III, SPF/PC, IBM OS/VS, JCL and CICS.

COMPUTER COMPUTATIONS/DATA PROCESSING—*Eight years.* Involved in all aspects of data retrieval from computations to design.

MATHEMATICAL—*Five years.* Performed daily algebraic and trigonometric calculations.

TEAMWORK—*Eight years.* Effectively and cooperatively worked in a fast-paced, demanding environment with all members of a surveying crew, and interacted with various executive key personnel.

ADDITIONAL QUALIFICATIONS—Demonstrated ability to "debug" programs written by others. Developed training and instructional materials for software packages. Designed, set up and operated PC-based database for record keeping.

EDUCATION

SPOKANE TECHNICAL INSTITUTE, Spokane, Washington 2007
672-hour course in Computer Programming and Operations. State certified. Graduated with Honors. GPA: 3.67

WASHINGTON STATE UNIVERSITY, Seattle, Washington 2005
Completed 15 semester hours in Computer Science which included courses in Computer Networking.

SEATTLE SCHOOL OF SURVEYING & MAPPING, Seattle, Washington 2003
Certificate for 1600-hour program.

EMPLOYMENT BACKGROUND

Party Chief for the following companies:
Avery Structures, Inc., Spokane, Washington, 2003–2008
Centennial Engineering, Seattle, Washington, 2000–2003
J.R. Developers, Tacoma, Washington, 1998–2000
Al Messahaq/ARAMCO, Saudi Arabia, 1994–1998

REFERENCES

Professional references will be provided upon request.

Mary C. Barnes

5343 Van Nuys Boulevard, Van Nuys, CA 91401   (318) 555-1354, mcbarnes@yahoo.com

OBJECTIVE

A position with an advertising agency where a sense of responsibility, an ability to work as a team member in groups, and marketing and communication skills are assets.

MAJOR WORK EXPERIENCE

Administrative Management

Hired, trained, and supervised data processing staff of ten. Managed office for national software development firm. In one year, reduced employee turnover in data processing department by 10%.

Public Relations

Prepared press releases and worked with media, brought regional recognition to new software program. Planned and coordinated monthly sales seminars and semi-annual conventions.

Advertising/Promotional

Designed and administrated newspaper, radio, and poster distribution for the introduction of new company programs and for the establishment of area sales centers.

Communication/Writing

Accurately reported sales activities to regional headquarters for all local sales/service centers. Created, edited, and printed revision of sales procedure manual, which directly contributed to a 25% increase in software sales.

EDUCATION

California State University, Los Angeles, CA
Bachelor of Science degree in Business Administration, minor in Computer Science.

Computer Learning Center, Los Angeles, CA
Completed 900-hour course in Data Processing.

REFERENCES

Professional references available upon request.

Pamela J. Smith

904 East 42nd Street
Longmont, CO 80397

(303) 555-6332
pjsmith@mci2005.com

OBJECTIVE

A position in the Hotel/Motel industry, preferably in Room Division Management.
Five-Year Goal: Resident Manager

SUMMARY OF QUALIFICATIONS

ACCOUNTING—*Two Years*. Knowledge of basic fundamentals and hospitality accounting.

KEYBOARDING—*Two Years*. Earned an "A" in my classes with typing speed of over 50 words per minute in college and high school.

TEAMWORK—Through working experience, involved in teamwork in all positions.

COMMUNICATION—*One Year*. Answering phones, dealing with customers and problem solving at A-Advanced Communications Answering Service. Learned how to communicate with all kinds of people in many diverse situations.

EDUCATION

WESTWOOD COLLEGE OF TECHNOLOGY, Denver, Colorado. Earned Associate's degree in Hospitality Management. Major courses included accounting, supervision, purchasing, front office procedures, sanitation, professional communications and law.

THOMPSON VALLEY HIGH SCHOOL—Earned diploma; completed all major subjects such as English, algebra, accounting, and science.

EMPLOYMENT BACKGROUND

Marriott Hotel, Fort Collins, Colorado. *Public Attendant*, 2005–Present

A-Advanced Communications Answering Service, Denver, Colorado. *Telephone Operator*, 2003–2005

Boyers Donuts, Loveland, Colorado. *Cashier/Counter Help*, 2001–2003

Myers Floor Covering, Lakewood, Colorado. *Sales Help*, 2000–2001

REFERENCES

Available upon request

Dale Merriman

2230 Hayes Street, Dallas, TX 75234   (214) 555-8965 dmerriman@earthlink.net

Objective

A long-term computer-aided drafting position with an architectural firm that values attention to detail, teamwork, and good communication skills.

Long-Term Goals

Management in a Drafting and Design firm and continued education resulting in the acquisition of an architect's license.

Education

Dallas School of Drafting & Design, Dallas, Texas
Associate's degree in Architectural Drafting, Graduate: 2008

Vrain Valley High School, Arlington, Texas
Graduate: 2004. Completed four semesters of basic drafting and design.

Employment History

Repair Order Booker/General Office, *Miner Lincoln Mercury*
Dallas, Texas. 2009 to present

Service Advisor/Dispatcher for the following companies:
Glenn Taylor Ford, Dallas, Texas 2002–2004
Dallas Hyundai Daihatsu, Arlington, Texas 2000–2002

Summary of Qualifications

Computer-Aided Drafting
Certified in AutoCAD. Experience with 2D, 3D, AutoLISP, and AutoCAD MNU.

Teamwork, Quality Control, Time Management
Seven years as team leader for four to fifteen technicians organizing, assigning and ensuring timely and proper completion of automotive repairs within estimated cost.

Attention to Detail, Organization, Administration
Seven years controlling all aspects of as many as 60 different jobs in any given day. Details included initial contact with customers to determine needed services, estimation of cost for those services, and sales of the services to customers both on the phone and in person. Acquired parts and assigned personnel to complete repairs in the time promised to customer.

Mary Groetken (Gret'ken)

633 North La Brea Avenue   (213) 555-4122
Los Angeles, CA 90036   marygroetken@pacbell.com

Objective: A position as a Medical Transcriptionist, preferably in Radiology or Pathology.

Summary of Qualifications

Computer Applications

Working knowledge of Life 70, CICS, WordPerfect, Quattro Pro, Excel, MS-DOS, and Medisoft if installed on IBM-compatible hardware.

Mathematical/Accounting

Processed payments from customers and adjusted financial records.

Quality Control

Responsible for checking accuracy and quality of work done by others and then returning errors to workers for corrections.

Communication

Responded to telephone calls and letters, then supplied required information to customers.

Training

Trained other employees for various positions. Also wrote procedures for employee training manuals.

Teamwork

Have diverse experience working with department managers, supervisors, fellow employees, and customers.

Education

Los Angeles College of Medical Transcription, Los Angeles, California.

Graduate: 2008, Associate's degree in Medical Transcription.

Awards: Director's List (GPA of 3.7 and above), Perfect Attendance.

Courses: Advanced Medical Terminology, Advanced Transcription (Radiology, Pathology, Cardiology, Gastrointestinal, Orthopedics), Computer Applications (MS-DOS, WordPerfect, Medisoft, and Excel).

Employment History

Self-Employed, Los Angeles, California. Three years, managed mail distribution business.

National Farmer's Insurance Company, Long Beach, California
Ten years in the following positions: Endorsement Specialist, Customer Service, Quality Control, Cash Control, Utility and Filing.

Norman Stevenson

50126 Road 24, South Bend, IN 46515   *(219) 555-1122 • ns3421@juno.com*

OBJECTIVE

A position in the Mechanical Drafting field with an emphasis on Computer-Aided drafting and the potential for advancement into design and development.

EDUCATION

Associate's degree in Mechanical Engineering, Indianapolis, IN
ETI Technical Institute, Graduate: 2008

Courses in the following areas:

Mechanical Drafting: Machine Design, Dimensioning and Tolerancing, Manufacturing Processes, Fasteners, Power Transmission, Descriptive Geometry, Piping, Wiring Schematics.

CAD (AutoCAD): Basic and advanced drawing, layers, blocks, attributes, 3D wireframe and surfacing, solid modeling, AutoLISP programming, designing menus, MS-DOS, batch files.

Math & Design: Algebra, trigonometry, machine design (statics and strengths of materials).

PROFESSIONAL PROFILE

- Experience in Mechanical Drafting and Design
- Leadership qualities: Served as Vice President on Board of Directors for Farmland Co-op, Fort Wayne, Indiana.
- Able to complete projects under pressure, maintained high grade point average at ETI Technical Institute and successfully operated my own farming business.

RELATED EXPERIENCE

Successfully developed conceptual design of equipment trailers. Redesigned various farm equipment; also designed and built a champion stock car.

EMPLOYMENT HISTORY

Owner/Operator—Stevenson Farms, South Bend, Indiana 2005–2008
Board of Directors—Farmland Co-op, South Bend, Indiana 1998–2005

ACADEMIC HONORS

Honors student with GPA of 3.88/4.0
Dean's list of Scholastic Excellence: 2006–2008
National Honor Society, Alpha Beta Kappa: 2007

EDNA L. WYCLIFF

4589 North Hillside, Topeka, KS 66609

(316) 555-9022

ednawycliff@yahoo.com

Education

WICHITA TECHNICAL COLLEGE
Automotive Technician
Associate's degree, 2008

KANSAS STATE UNIVERSITY
Completed 3 years of Industrial
Technology: Plastics & Metals Technology
and Fabrication, Electronics, Computer
Drafting, Physics and Mechanics of Materials.

Summary of Skills

Equipment: Alignment Racks, Scopes,
VAT 40-60, Brake Lathes, Valve Grinding
Equipment, Turning Lathes, Mills,
Welding Equipment, Fork Lifts.

Computer: ACAD, WordPerfect,
Macintosh, TWIN, Basic, Al-Data Automotive.
Type 45 wpm.

Automotive Repair Skills:
ASE Certified, Engine Repair,
Brakes, Suspensions and
Steering, Air Conditioning and Heating.

Special Accomplishments

State of Kansas Emissions,
Technician's License

Honor Society—four years

All-Conference Honorable Mention—
Basketball
State Qualifier—Pole Vault

Work Experience

Emissions technician, bottom
tech, upper bay tech, sales
Phillips 66 Fast Lube,
Wichita, Kansas 9/06 to present

General merchandise clerk,
floor care, shelf stocker,
checker, order writer
Safeway Stores, Topeka, Kansas
2003–2006

All-purpose clerk, stocker,
checker, order writer
Beavers Market, Topeka, Kansas
2001–2003

Field applicator, field scout
and advisor, warehouse supervisor
Morley Ag Services, Topeka, Kansas
2000–2001

References

Provided upon request.

Phillips 66,
Fast Lube Training Certificate

Future Business Leaders
of America—two years

Joyce Challenger

27932 Cactus Lane   (520) 555-2760
Tucson, AZ 85719   joycechallenger@azrepublic.net

OBJECTIVE

To work in the computer networking field where the ability to work as a team member,
a sense of responsibility, and excellent communication skills are assets.

EDUCATION

Associate of Applied Science degree in Computer Networking
Arizona Technical Institute, Phoenix, AZ
Graduate: 2008
Associate of Science degree, Northeastern College, Villanova, PA
Graduate: 2002

SUMMARY OF QUALIFICATIONS

- **Operating Systems:** DOS, UNIX/LINUX, NetWare, Windows NT Server

- **Implementing and Supporting the Functions and Administration of Network
  Information Systems:** Included planning, configuring and installing file server, work
  station, and print server in the local area environment.

- **Networks:** Peer-to-peer and server-based network connections using NetBEUI,
  IPX/SPX, and TCP/IP transport protocols.

ADDITIONAL SKILLS

- Microsoft Word, Excel, Access, PowerPoint, Windows, Technical Writing

AWARDS

Alpha Beta Kappa   •   Dean's List for Academic Excellence   •   3.9 GPA

EMPLOYMENT HISTORY

Office Edge Training Center, Tucson, AZ, current position
Green Valley Mountain School, Tucson, AZ, 2004–2007
Better Homes & Gardens Real Estate, Phoenix, AZ, 2002–2004
Interlink Products Corporation, Villanova, PA 2000–2002

7854 East Martin Luther King Blvd.
Aurora, CO 80010
October 15, 2008

Mr. Dennis Kelly
MAC Tools Corporation
1757 Hoyt Street
Lakewood, CO 80215

Dear Mr. Kelly:

Having recently earned my Associate's degree in Occupational Sciences of Automotive Technology
from the Westwood College of Technology and graduating with a GPA of 4.0 has fueled my years
of interest in the field of automotive technology. This accelerated education, coupled with an
existing desire to be employed in the automotive industry, makes me eager to be placed in a position
with your company.

The attached resume summarizes my experience and education for you. Westwood College offers,
to all graduates the opportunity to receive lifetime training so I can keep current with new material and procedures. This benefit will be an asset to your company because I will have ongoing
retraining in my field at no cost to you.

As for my other qualifications, completing EDGE training has taught me diagnostic procedures
for automotive repair, and I am ASE certified with a clean, no-ticket driving record. I already
have most of the tools needed to begin my career, and I am in the process of purchasing
more diagnostic equipment.

When you review the enclosed resume and see that I match the qualifications that you ask of your
automotive technicians, I believe you will consider me for a position with MAC Tools Corporation.
I look forward to meeting with you and becoming part of your team. You can contact me at the
number below between 5 and 10 p.m. weekdays and all day on the weekends. If I'm not there,
please leave a message with my voice messaging service. Please do not contact my present employer
as he is not aware of my decision to leave, and I want to give two weeks' notice at the appropriate
time.

Sincerely,

Harold Blake

Harold Blake
(303) 555-1221
blake56@yahoo.com

Enclosed: Resume

5094 Osceola Street
Westminster, CO 80030-3173
May 20, 2008

Michelle Graves, Legal Administrator
Smith & Graves, P.C.
10742 West 120th Avenue
Broomfield, CO 80020

RE: Network Administrator/Desktop Support Specialist

Dear Ms. Graves:

I am writing to respond to your advertisement for a Network Administrator and Desktop Support Specialist which appeared in the Sunday *Denver Post*, May 15, 2008. I am impressed with your firm's prestigious reputation and long-standing commitment to client service.

The attached resume formally presents my qualifications. However, the personal attributes that I am most proud of are my initiative and drive. I accomplish what is required, correctly and on time. I know how to juggle a multitude of tasks—some critical, some routine— while remaining courteous and professional. I have combined my long experience resolving customer challenges with newly developed technical skills. My goal is to provide technical support for customers and coworkers as they negotiate through complex and at times mystifying computer network problems.

My unique combination of education, training, and experience allows me to offer your firm great value as an employee. I look forward to meeting with you to discuss the specific requirements for this position and my ability to meet them. Please contact me at your convenience at the number below to schedule an interview. Thank you for taking the time to consider me as an applicant for this position.

Sincerely,

Mark T Wheeling Jr.

Mark T. Wheeling, Jr.
(303) 555-9023
mtw@uswest.net

Attached: Resume, reference letters

6998 Pearl Street
Dallas, TX 75207
June 22, 2008

Randolph Minnick
South Polar Heating & Air Conditioning
4323 Maple Avenue
Dallas, Texas 75235

Dear Mr. Minnick:

I am most interested in obtaining an HVAC position with your company. With my training and interest in Heating, Air Conditioning and Ventilation Serving, I believe that your company would be an ideal place for me to begin. I believe that I can be a key person in the continued success of your reputable company. The enclosed resume provides the information detailing my background and abilities. I am confident that upon review of my qualifications, you will find that I am a strong candidate for your next available opening.

As my resume indicates, I have just completed a program at the American Trades Institute specializing in Heating, Ventilation, Air Conditioning, and Refrigeration. My abilities and potential for success can be greatly broadened by securing a challenging position with your company. What may not be adequately reflected in the resume are my computer skills, mechanical aptitude, and high level of energy and professional work ethic. Fast-paced environments and pressure are no stranger to me; I function well under both.

During the course of my studies, I was educated in HVAC maintenance and have knowledge and strong skills in refrigeration systems, air conditioners, gas/forced air furnaces, and electronic control systems. I also earned my Universal CFC certification in refrigeration. At this point in my career, I am seeking an opportunity that will allow me to fully utilize my education and skills, as well as gain new knowledge in the field.

I would consider it an honor to meet with you to discuss your requirements as related to my qualifications for the position of HVAC Technician. If at that time you believe we are a "match," I believe we could look forward to a long and mutually profitable relationship. I look forward to hearing from you, at your earliest convenience, with reference to a position with South Polar. You can contact me at the number below or at my e-mail address: rwallace@yahoo.com.

Sincerely,

Robert Wallace

Robert Wallace
(214) 555-4556
rwallace@yahoo.com

Enclosed: Resume and reference letters

1003 Massachusetts Avenue
Boston, MA 02115
August 23, 2008

Mr. Tom Flynn
Flynn's Graphics, Inc.
90 Marlborough Street
Boston, MA 02116

Dear Mr. Flynn:

At the forefront of every successful visual undertaking, whether it's a magazine cover, a business brochure, or an entire ad campaign, there should be a top-of-the-line graphic designer. As a graphic designer in the field, I am confident that I can provide you with ideas and images that can bring unquestionable recognition and extraordinary results.

I have seven years' experience (noted in my resume) in digital typesetting, electronic publishing, and computer graphic design. I am a proficient user of major computer page-layout, image creation/editing, illustration, and word processing software on both Macintosh and PC (DOS- and Windows-based) platforms. This experience includes knowledge and proficiency with PageMaker, QuarkXPress, Photoshop, and Illustrator. So as you can see, I am very familiar with all aspects of the graphic design process.

Self-motivation is one of my strong points. I worked full-time and attended college at the same time, earning my degree with a grade point average of 3.7. I have worked in several professional and management positions, and because of my skills in communications and dealing with people, I was considered a valuable team member.

At your earliest convenience, I would very much appreciate an interview with you to discuss how my qualifications could contribute to the continued success of Flynn's Graphics, Inc. I will bring my portfolio at that time to show you my designs.

Sincerely,

Steven Marks

Steven Marks
Residence: (617) 555-8090
Pager: (617) 555-4455
steven_marks@hotmail.com

320 West 31st Street
New York, NY 10001
May 6, 2009

R. Rudy Lee, President
Traphagen Marketing & Advertising
257 Park Avenue South
New York, NY 10010

Dear Mr. Lee:

Our mutual friend, Karne Scott, suggested I write you about possible employment with your firm. Because of my training and interest in marketing and all types of advertising, in addition to your reputation for creative and innovative design, I am especially excited at the prospect of going to work for Traphagen Marketing & Advertising.

I will be graduating June 12 with a Master's degree in Advertising Design & Technical Illustration from New York State University. I made the Dean's list this year and was vice president of the University Advertising Club at New York State for the past two years. I promoted the club's membership program, which netted 50 new members, and I was responsible for the design, layout, and production of the advertising and marketing for an on-campus career fair.

As you can see from the enclosed resume, I worked in retail management at Conte Jewelers while I was attending the university. I began as a clerk and after six months was promoted to assistant manager. In this position, I had full responsibility for the advertising campaigns and the marketing strategies for new jewelry lines. This included complete layout and design, market surveys, and budget allocations. I believe that my education, coupled with this experience, would enable me to be a contributing member of your marketing and advertising team.

I'm excited about the prospect of discussing employment with Traphagen and look forward to meeting with you at your earliest convenience. You may contact me at the number below.

Sincerely,

Carolyn B. Greene

Carolyn B. Greene
(212) 555-5225
cbg118@aol.com
Enclosure: Resume, design samples

12103 Melody Drive, #404
Westminster, CO 80233
July 16, 2009

Emily Griffith Opportunity School
1250 Welton Street
Denver, CO 80221

Attention: Director of Education

I am most interested in exploring the possibility of obtaining a teaching position with Emily Griffith Opportunity School. Instructing English, Composition, Business Correspondence, or Career Skills would be ideal; however, I am open to any discipline that you believe I am qualified to teach.

As reflected in the enclosed resume, my experience and education, with a concentration in basic skills and career development instruction, provide a solid background in my field. I believe my qualifications, in addition to my intense love of teaching and a strong commitment to being an understanding, caring teacher, meet the requirements of an Emily Griffith instructor.

I have taken the liberty of including a few of the reference letters that I have received over the past ten years from my students, coworkers, and administrative staff. I believe you will agree that they reflect my commitment to being the kind of teacher who is dedicated to helping students recognize their educational and personal goals.

Thank you for considering my application for a teaching position at your school. I would appreciate an opportunity to discuss with you, in person, how I could become part of your teaching staff. You may contact me at the number below any time of day. If I am not there, please leave a message, and I will return your call promptly.

Sincerely,

Judy L. Dally

Judy L. Dally
(303) 555-0367
dally@idcomm.com

Enclosure: Resume, reference letters

16205 Riverside Lane
Brighton, CO 80601
October 16, 2009

Mr. John Smith
Main-Tec, Inc.
2412 Rose Street
Suite 102
Honolulu, Hawaii 96819

Dear Mr. Smith:

I am a recent Electronic Technician graduate of the Westwood College of Technology in Denver, Colorado. I am interested in employment in the Hawaiian Islands. Because of my background experience and education, I would be very interested in any appropriate available positions within Main-Tec, Inc. My research of the islands indicates a rapidly growing electronics industry, and I would like to be a part of that development.

My experience and education are summarized for you in the enclosed resume. Following are a few of my skills that could be of use to your company. Knowledge of and proficiency with foreign languages allow me to relate to various cultural differences, which is an advantage in customer relations, a skill so necessary in field work. I have excellent mathematical and logical aptitude, which enables me to analyze situations and to determine efficient solutions. My programming experience on IBM and MacIntosh computers would be an asset in that I can readily troubleshoot and repair many kinds of systems. 1 am proficient in MS-DOS, UNIX/LINUX, and NT and am familiar with Java and Applescript. One final advantage to hiring me is that since I am a recent graduate, I am still accustomed to a learning environment and can be trained quickly, therefore saving you time and money.

Thank you for your time in examining my qualifications; I am looking forward to the opportunity of a possible future with Main-Tec, Inc. I will be in Honolulu the first week in November and will contact you then. Should you need to reach me before that date, I am available at the above address, or I will gladly accept a collect call at the number below.

Sincerely,

Richard Martinez

Richard Martinez
(303) 547-2183
rmartinez@attglobal.net

7816 Montview Drive
Orange, CA 92669
June 15, 2009

Stevenson's Office Machines
4500 Ocean Boulevard
Suite 2103
Long Beach, CA 98022

Attention: Data Processing Manager

The *Los Angeles Times* recently reported that Stevenson's Office Machines is building a
new data processing center in the Compton area. I would like to apply for a position as a
computer programmer and have enclosed a resume for your consideration.

I am a recent graduate of Systems Programming Development Institute with an
Associate's degree in Computer Science. In addition to taking a broad range of courses in
many business-related languages (noted in my resume), I was a tutor and consultant at the
college for the students having difficulty with those languages. Most recently, I have been
doing volunteer work in programming for the local high schools here in Orange County.
I believe that you would find my skills valuable in assisting you in getting the center off
and running.

I will be happy to meet with you at your earliest convenience and will provide any additional information you may need. You can contact me at (714) 555-6781 any time; I have
an answering machine and check my messages regularly. In addition, you may e-mail me
at ghrowlands@home.com.

Sincerely,

Gena H. Rowlands

Gena H. Rowlands
Enclosures: Resume, reference letters

5336 West Tejone Street
Lakewood, CO 80333
October 28, 2009

Ms. Joan Fredericksen
Itel Corporation
1650 Stout Street, # 207
Denver, CO 80206

Dear Ms. Fredericksen:

I recently earned my Associate's degree in Electronics Technology from ITT Technical Institute in Denver, Colorado. This formal education, along with several years of great interest and devoted pursuit of computer systems, makes me eager to be placed in a position you may find suitable with your corporation.

I have enclosed a resume which summarizes my experience and education, yet some, I believe, require further explanation. For example, because I fluently speak three languages, I understand and respect cultural variety. This skill can be an asset with customers as well as fellow workers. I am also flexible, yet reliable.

As for my other qualifications, I especially like working with MS-DOS, which the advertisement in the *Rocky Mountain News* indicated that your corporation uses extensively. I am also experienced with digital/analog microprocessor-based circuitry. Furthermore, because your corporation manufactures telecommunications hardware, perhaps you should know that I am knowledgeable and interested in this branch of technology. In addition to these skills, I have an Amateur Radio license, and I actively participate in various forms of radio communications including Morse code, satellite, and packet radio.

Thank you for considering my qualifications. I look forward to the opportunity of talking with you in person about how I could become employed with Itel Corporation.

Sincerely,

Daniel Simone

Daniel Simone
(303) 555-9350
d1336@juno.com

Enclosure: Resume

16307 West Alaska Place
Lincoln, NE 68508-2478
May 18, 2009

Dale Skyhorn
Tri-City Design Corporation
Post Office Box 80245
Omaha, NE 68105

Dear Mr. Skyhorn:

The key to successful organizations is quality personnel. I would like to contribute to your success. Please accept the enclosed resume as application for the position of mechanical drafter with Tri-City Design.

As you can see from my professional background, I have extensive experience in the design, layout, and production of sheet metal fabrication. My current position demands leadership ability as well as interpersonal skills and comprehensive decision making. I am responsible for the production and design of all sheet metal fabricated parts. I also analyze and report on the progress and quality of each project and purchase all raw materials. Creativity and self-motivation are two of my strongest suits. Across the United States, I have established many successful relationships with vendors and suppliers.

Over the past eight years, I have gained invaluable experience at my present position with Norwest Systems, but I am now ready for new challenges that will expand my professional potential. I would very much like to speak with you about opportunities within Tri-City Design. I will be in contact with you within the next week; however, please feel free to contact me (discreetly) at work (402) 555-1587 or leave a message at my home, and I will return your call. Also, please consider contacting me via e-mail at mcordlin@yahoo.com; I check my messages daily.

Thank you for your consideration. I look forward to meeting with you.

Sincerely,

Micheal Cordlin

Micheal Cordlin
(402) 555-9034

Works Consulted

AARP Bulletin. 601 E St. N.W., Washington, DC 20049; various volumes.

AARP The Magazine. 601 E St. N.W., Washington, DC 20049; various volumes.

Allen, Robert G. *Creating Wealth*. 2nd ed. New York: Simon & Schuster, 1983.

Baldrige, Letitia. *Letitia Baldrige's Complete Guide to Executive Manners*. New York: Rawson Associates, 1985.

Brandt, Rhonda, and Barry L. Reece. *Effective Human Relations in Organizations*. 4th ed. Boston: Houghton Mifflin Company, 1990.

BusinessWeek, "The New Global Job Shift, Cover Image: Is Your Job Next?" February 3, 2003.

Challenger, James E. Job Decision Isn't Just About the Money. Available at: www.suntimes.com/output/challenger/chat, January 16, 2000.

Cohen, Herb. *You Can Negotiate Anything*. New York: Bantam Books, 1980.

Denver Post, The. Jobs and Careers, Classified section. Denver: various editions.

Dikel, Margaret Riley. *The Guide to Internet Job Searching*. NTC/Contemporary Publishing, 1998–1999.

Graber, Steven. *The Everything Get-a-Job Book*. Avon, MA: Adams Media Corp., 2000.

Gray, James, Jr. *The Winning Image*. New York: American Management Association, 1982.

Greenleaf III, Clinton T., and Stefani Schaefer. *Attention to Detail: A Woman's Guide to Professional Appearance and Conduct*. Chesterland, OH: Greenleaf Enterprises, 2000.

Herzberg, Frederick. *Work and the Nature of Man*. Cleveland, OH: World Publishing, 1966.

Lynch, Richard L., Herbert L. Ross, Ralph D. Wray, and Robert J. Welch. *Introduction to Marketing*. New York: McGraw-Hill, 1984.

MSN Careers. Available at: http://msn.careerbuilder.com. Various articles, July 2004.

MSN Money. Available at: http://moneycentral.msn.com. Various articles, July 2004.

Nemnich, Mary B., and Fred E. Jandt. *Cyberspace Job Search Kit 2001–2002: The Complete Guide to Online Job Seeking and Career Information*. Indianapolis, IN: JIST Works, 2001.

Occupational Outlook Handbook. U.S. Department of Labor, Bureau of Labor Statistics. Washington, DC: Government Printing Office, 2000.

O'Malley, Michael. *Are You Paid What You're Worth?* New York: Broadway Books, 1998.

Pulliman Weston, Liz. Your Money Message Board: How Bad Credit Can Cost You a Job. Available at: http://moneycentral.msn.com, February 7, 2004.

Reader's Digest, Box 100, Pleasantville, NY 10572–0100; various articles, April 2004, 2008.

Reiss, Steven. Testing Methods: Reiss Profile of Fundamental Goals and Motivational Sensitivities. Available at: grow.up.managementberatungGmbH.

Rocky Mountain News. Careers, Classified section, Denver: various editions.

Rosenbloom, Jerry. *The Handbook of Employee Benefits*. Vol. 1, 3rd ed. Homewood, IL: Dow Jones–Irwin, 1984.

Seligman, Martin. Available at: Wikipedia.org/wikiMartin_Seligman, April 10, 2008.

Straits, Don. CEO and Dragon Slayer, Corporate Warriors. E-mail: don@corporatewarriors.com.

Standard Life Investments, Limited. *Gallup Interviews*, April 11, 2008.

Terrell, Kenneth. "When Experience Counts, Older Workers are Finding a Welcome in the Job Market." *U.S. News & World Report*, March 1, 2007.

Turner, Joe. Is a Video Resume for You? Available at: msn.career builder.com, July 6, 2007.

U.S. News & World Report. New York: various editions.

Walker Information Global Network. 2000 Walker Information, Inc. Available at: www.walkerinfo.com/globalnetwork.

Index